HOUSES
OF
GOD

HOUSES OF GOD

by

Jeannette Mirsky

The University of Chicago Press
Chicago and London

The University of Chicago Press, Chicago 60637
The University of Chicago Press, Ltd., London
Copyright 1965 by Jeannette Mirsky in all countries
of the International Copyright Union.
All rights reserved
Published 1966 by Constable and Company Ltd.
Phoenix Edition 1976
Printed in the United States of America
International Standard Book Number: 0-226-53184-8
Library of Congress Catalog Card Number: 76-1536

To the memory of
my husband
Edward Bellamy Ginsburg

AUTHOR'S NOTE

This book is designed to give through pictures and accompanying text a sampling of how men have envisioned the houses of their gods. Though the book deals with religious buildings, it is neither a book about religion as religion, nor one about architecture as architecture. It is, rather, a book about the various attitudes with which men have approached their gods and how such attitudes have shaped their places of worship.

The familiar masterpieces are included—it is impossible to omit the examples of ripe perfection—but alongside are other examples, less well known. Making a selection from the glories and grandeur which exist in vast number has forced me to be ruthless and permitted me to be personal.

In the preparation of this book I have received personal help and encouragement and valuable professional assistance. The book and I have benefited greatly from the kindnesses and knowledge so generously given. In particular I should like to thank my good friends Harry and Cecile Starr, Catherine Davis, Joan Daves, Marie Rodell, Louise Levinson, John T. Harmon, and my sister-in-law, Hazel Mirsky. I should like to mention the special help that I have had from the late Mrs. Rebecca Tcherikower of the Yivo Archives and from Mrs. Marianne Adelmann, who located many of the pictures I asked for. The phrases quoted in chapter III are from Dr. Stella Kramrisch, whose studies of Indian art and architecture—so cogent in their argument, so elegant in their phrasing—influenced me profoundly.

J.M

Contents

INTRODUCTION

Houses of God are – in Yeats's phrase – "artifices of eternity." Everywhere we find arresting evidence, from all times, of man's acknowledgment of a power greater than human. And whether the god – or goddess – is found in a mountain, a stone, a bog, a tree, the inmost recess of a cave, or lodged in a temple or a church, the deity's presence sanctifies the place. Such sacred sites are a visible expression of man's intense wonder and faith as well as his everlasting cry for help and hope.

From the very earliest times, the houses of the gods are proof of man's abiding effort to explain the mysteries of birth and life and death, increase and regeneration; to define behavior as good or evil; to mold attitudes and to answer the immemorial questions of what? how? why? and wherefore? However these questions are answered, in however different a cultural idiom, they voice the stab and sweep of human emotions, and are shaped by visions and hopes. Each place of worship can be seen as an attempt to translate myth and symbol, dogma and ritual, into earth and stone and wood.

Gods are not approached in an offhand manner, and their dwelling places are characterized by the serious, vital, sometimes lofty, sometimes dangerous purpose to which they are consecrated. Many such places are stupendous, overwhelming the eye and informing the imagination. And so it should be. A monumental edifice proclaims that its creation has mobilized the human resources of an entire society for generations: that beyond the satisfaction of their biological needs, the time and strength of many individuals throughout their lifetimes have been channeled into a nonutilitarian sacred task. Indeed the existence in every land of such a great number of mighty religious sanctuaries and ceremonial centers is a witness to more than organized, large-scale, protracted labor; it suggests, perhaps, that man stands apart from all other creatures not only as a toolmaker and word-maker, but as a worshiper and temple builder as well.

Lately scholars have been providing us with evidence of the many sources from which our science and technology have drawn their ideas and inventions. Similarly, in this panorama of religious buildings, we may observe the flow and the flowering of religious concepts and architectural motifs which preceded and often molded those of our own day. In the past, as the human family spread over the earth, living in isolated units with few outside contacts, the basic concepts of religion and their architectural expression grew more diverse. Today, as the world grows smaller, this process has reversed itself: the ancient isolated beliefs are disappearing, and more and more religious feeling is seen as belonging to all mankind. To this new understanding the Chapel at the United Nations is dedicated; within its walls every faith and every people may worship and meditate. The chapel is the embodiment of the political idea of One World, stated in the spiritual terms of the brotherhood of man.

HOUSES
OF
GOD

The towers have never been finished,
save as time finishes things, by perpetuat-
ing their incompleteness. There is some-
thing right in old monuments that have
been wrong for centuries.

HENRY JAMES

THE BEGINNING According to our present knowledge, man's awareness of superhuman forces began in the dim period of the last interglacial age when a new human type, the beetle-browed Neanderthal Man, emerged. His skeletal remains show that he buried his dead according to ritual, but more than that—what rites and ceremonies attended the burials, what ideas and myths and cults he might have associated with death—we do not know. The inhabitants of his graves still keep their secrets.

But in every civilization we know of, death is related to religion; the funerary observances imply a relationship among the dead, the quick, and the supernatural. Was the grave a sacred no man's land between the living, in this world, and the world of the spirits? Or did the dead themselves hold the balance of power, the power for good, the power to harm? We can only ask questions.

In the final stages of the last glacial age, Neanderthal Man's long tenure in Western Europe ended. He was replaced by different groups of *Homo sapiens*, our true ancestors, who, with their new tools and more specialized techniques, ushered in the late Paleolithic period. The newcomers bequeathed us more than their inventions of the cutting knife and chisel (made first in flint) and the mechanical principle of the lever; they also left us the earliest places of worship we know to have been touched by the work of man.

The full meaning of the miraculously preserved art of the Ice Age caves still eludes us, and we shall never know the words and dances, the rites and practices associated with it. However, we can see that the frescoes celebrate abundant life, and evidence shows that game was easily obtained everywhere. An economy of plenty gave these hunters leisure to explore their humanity and its spiritual potentialities.

In the caves, the location of the astonishing engravings, paintings, and sculpture is in itself significant: the decorated walls and ceilings are always removed from the places for living. Within the vast, meandering caves the hunter-artists selected sites which were dark and silent, inhospitable, and sometimes almost inaccessible. More than anything else, the location of the friezes and symbols tells us that these were not decorations for the houses of mere men: they are glorified sanctuaries. Here we have the impressive beginning of man's heroic devotion to works not directly related to material needs.

We have found no trace of any European sanctuaries between the time of the Paleolithic cathedral caves and the building of the later megalithic tombs. These holy sites of an extraordinary funerary cult were, it would seem, related to what is called ancestor

1

worship. From grave goods and food offerings left at shrines within the tombs, we know that these were centers of worship, places to which men came to pray, places in which were housed the deified spirits of their ancestors.

Whether the idea of encasing collective burials in huge stone slabs reached Europe by way of Malta in the central Mediterranean or by way of Spain has not been determined; but the resulting megalithic tombs form a remarkable example of successive cultures. The tombs are various in form. In those called "passage graves," the chamber which contains the dead—it can be circular or rectangular, flat-roofed or corbeled—was entered through a narrow passage. The "gallery grave" or "long cist" was a single long, rectangular compartment with no passageway. The distinguishing characteristic of both types was their use of enormous stone slabs for walls and roof. We are now fairly certain that the differences between the types of tombs stemmed from religious differences—matters of dogma or ritual—not differences of architectural or artistic conception. The immense human labor required to collect, move, and raise stones that weighed many tons, and finally to cover the whole tomb with earth, must have mobilized the strength of entire communities. How basic and powerful must have been the emotion that drove the builders!

Shortly after 2300 B.C., men in Sicily and Sardinia, southern France, Portugal, and Spain seem to have been engaged in the mass production of monumental mausoleums. Then from the centers of the Iberian peninsula the idea of megalithic tombs was spread by sea routes northward to Brittany and the British Isles, and eastward to the lands bordering on the Baltic. So irresistible, so contagious was the practice that within three hundred years megalithic graves had become part of the landscape. A common belief united the coastal dwellers of Europe in a common religious tradition that cut across tribal barriers and differences of culture and language. Twenty-five hundred years later, the saints of the Celtic Church, following the same routes and within sight of the earlier landmarks, brought to the same lands the Christian Gospel and the knowledge of Christian architecture. And as the saints were committed to sectarian differences and architectural preferences, so the faith of the megalith builder rested on the virtues he attributed to the type of tomb he believed in. The pre-eminence and magnificence of the passage graves in northwestern Europe speak of the ardent faith, the enterprise, and the success of those dedicated to this type of plan.

Similarly, in the New World, religious cults whose messages we do not know, but whose appeal and galvanic effect have left astonishing ceremonial centers, spread rapidly over wide areas, carrying their impulses into different cultures. This now seems the most likely explanation for the distinctive art and building styles of the first prominent culture in Peru (the Chavín horizon, about 850–500 B.C.) and the otherwise unrelated Effigy Mounds (about 500 A.D.) and Temple Mounds (about 1000 A.D.) scattered throughout the United States.

We need not condescend to early man. Like us he was concerned with the ultimate realities of life and death, human fertility, the daily struggle for survival, and the ever-present threat of extinction. Faith created myths, images, and sanctuaries to deal with fear and wonder, longing and hope.

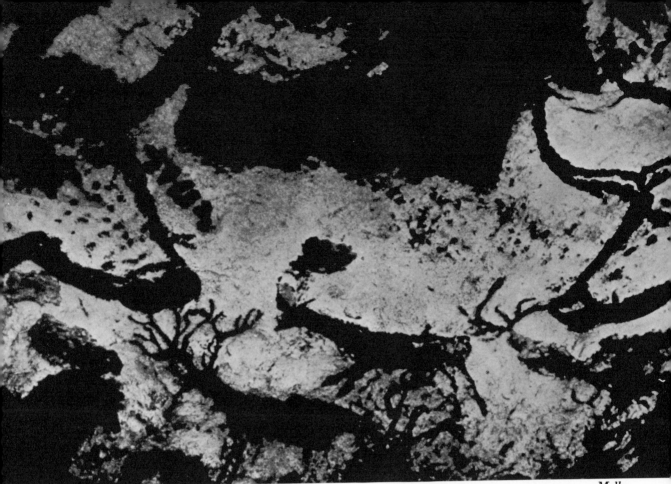

Hall of the Bulls, Lascaux   *Mella*

Plan of Lascaux

Great Hall of the Bulls

Lascaux, in southwestern France, was discovered in 1940. It has been called the "Sistine Chapel of the Prehistoric." Some thirty thousand years ago man glorified on the walls of the Ice Age caves the prizes awaiting great hunters. On the uneven surfaces of caves that lead deep into the earth, the artist-hunters created a paean to plenty, cataloguing the animals on which they fed and feasted: bison, bulls, mammoths, wild horses, stags, reindeer, bears, and rhinoceroses. The enormous roundup seems to fill the silent air with the sound of animal hooves, animal noises, and heavy, labored breathing; the colors—the black of soot, the browns and reds of earth hues, and a light yellow—are still fresh and alive. The photograph above shows part of the scene painted on the left-hand wall of the Great Hall of the Bulls.

Venus of Laussel *Mella*

Los Millares, Almería *Mella*

The important center for the cult of the dead, at Los Millares in Almería, Spain, had sixty-five tombs. In the model above, we can see how the chamber was covered with carefully arranged stones which were then coated with tightly packed earth. At the entrance to the tomb was the space for the funerary rituals.

The Venus of Laussel, though only eighteen inches high, is monumental; big-breasted, big-hipped, she is fecundity. Symbol of all increase, animal, vegetable, and human, she reappears down the ages, the Great Mother whom Robert Graves has hailed,

> With so huge a sense
> Of her nakedly worn magnificence.

Aside from such sanctuaries as Lascaux and Laussel, created during the Ice Age, some thirty thousand years ago, we have no religious architecture more then six thousand years old. But structures serving the prehistoric cults of the dead were more than mere tombs. They were designed with altars, a clearly defined space for worshipers, and an aperture through which offerings were passed to the dead; they were furnished with grave goods, and sometimes other human beings were interred to serve the dead in the spirit world. Burials of such astonishing richness, as in the Royal Tombs at Ur, the mortuary monuments of Egypt, Syria, and, in Europe, the famous beehive "Tomb of Agamemnon" at Mycenae, imply that men who had importance in this world must make their entry into the next in the full pride of their earthly rank and possessions. It was to provide them with precious paraphernalia that societies were stimulated to produce their finest art and to store up wealth.

Aerial view of temples, Mnaidra, Malta

The famous megalithic "temples" at Mnaidra *(below, left)* show the mastery of these builders, who used colossal stones to form elegant and intricate chambers, each with its apse. Malta has been suggested as the bridge by which the collective burial cults of the Near East came into Europe.

Pitting certain surfaces of the rock, as at Hagar Qim, Malta, was an effective decorating technique. The entrance to the burial chamber was closed with a porthole slab which increased the temple's resemblance to a cave, natural or man-made.

Hagar Qim, Malta

Shrine tomb *(neveta)*, Minorca

Burial shrines in Minorca are known as *nevetas*. Within, the chamber is bottle-shaped, fairly long and narrow, widening out at the far end. It was wholly above ground.

Along the Brittany coast, the first landfall northward from the Iberian peninsula, is Europe's greatest concentration of megalithic graves. From the goods and furniture buried with the dead, we know that every variety of cultic tradition was represented. It is thought that a single dolmen might have been raised as a monument to commemorate a special sacrifice—a human sacrifice, perhaps.

Dolmens in Brittany

Photos: Mella

The gods in nature:

THE TIME OF THE GOLDEN BOUGH. The greatness Europe had achieved in Late Paleo-lithic times collapsed; Lascaux and Altamira had no true heir. But the gods men wor-shiped were still present. All nature was "possessed, pervaded, crowded with spiritual beings"; anything and everything on earth, below it, and above it could be and was singled out as the dwelling of a god. Hunting groups wandering into lands that showed no human footprint were free to let their imaginations and emotions dictate where the gods lived: mountains, rivers, stones (from pebbles to boulders), plants and trees, earth and air, clouds and winds, lightning, thunder, fire, birds and beasts and serpents: the list of places and objects harboring spirits was endless.

GREAT GODS DWELL IN STONES. Free-standing pillars, alone, grouped, or placed close to a temple, were venerated in very early times. The Canaanite stone at Hazor in northern Israel *(below, left)* was carved with hands raised to the sun. The custom of raising pillars was old five thousand years ago, when twin pillars were raised before the moon god's temple at Ur. In Egypt the obelisk stood for the sun god Amon-Ra (or Ra-Atum); according to Breasted its pyramidal capstone, the Ben-ben, originally occupied a sanc-tuary in the sun temple at Heliopolis. Jachin and Boaz were names given the pillars of Solomon's Temple. In the Indus Valley there were sacred pillars in pre-Aryan times.

"A savage forest of primitive stone pillars"—so the phallic stones at Byblos *(below, right)* have been described by Julian Huxley. Each one in this collection of pillars was a *mazzebah,* the Hebrew word for such holy pillars. Blood sacrifices were made before them. Pre-Mosaic practices centered on their worship. It may be thus that the transla-tors of the Bible introduced the word "rock"—not as a metaphor derived from nature but as an emotionally charged reference to the primitive awe a *mazzebah* inspired. Today at Mecca, devout Moslems circumambulate the Kaaba in which is set the holy Black Stone.

Canaanite stone, Hazor, discovered 1954   Obelisk temple, Byblos   *Parrish*

Lannoy

Stonehenge   *Fritz Henle*

Stonehenge *(above)* is one of Britain's finest sacred monuments and one of the two greatest pagan ones. (Avebury, nearby, is the other.) In its completed form Stonehenge marks the coming of the Bronze Age to Britain. The invaders who brought the first metal-working technique—an Indo-European group with a sky god— overthrew the "megalithic aristocracy" and freed the stone-using farmers and herders they had conquered from their "megalithic superstition." (Or, as stated another way by Jacquetta Hawkes, Stonehenge marks the triumph of a "barbaric Zeus over the ancient Earth Mother dear to the Neolithic peasantry.") The underground cults which accompanied the knowledge of agriculture and animal husbandry from the Fertile Crescent into northern Europe yielded to celestial gods.

Approached by a single avenue, the mighty ceremonial center is a vast circle clearly marked by a ditch. Within stood two circles of gigantic upright stones enclosing two horseshoe-shaped series of equally large standing stones. This final design was the result of changes and major additions. Archaeologists recognize a Stonehenge I, about 1800

7

B.C., a Stonehenge II, somewhat later, and three phases of a Stonehenge III, 1500–1400 B.C. We know much about this shrine, but there is more we do not know. We can discern its successive stages, measure the ditch and embankment that delimit its sacred space, trace where its two kinds of monolithic stones came from, suggest the overland and overwater paths by which these monsters were transported for two hundred miles, examine the contents of the Aubrey holes—the ring of fifty-six ritual pits placed inside the bank. But we do not know what genius created this noble monument and supervised its execution, or what ceremonies were performed, or what god lived there. Much, much later the Druids held their rituals here, but the shrine was already ancient.

We know that the great upright stones connected by lintels curved, doweled, and grooved to precise form were oriented to the solstices. Thus the tip of the large standing Heelstone, or Sunstone, received the first rays of the rising sun at the summer solstice. But Stonehenge's principal ceremony, it is thought, was the winter solstice. On that day, as the last rays of the setting sun shone through the mighty trilithon, the god passed through the door which led to his tomb in the Netherworld.

Passage grave, Denmark

Aistrup

Sacred lake
at Karnak

Viollet

In Denmark, on the island of Møn, intact after four thousand years, is the passage grave known as "King Asger's Barrow" *(above)*, one of the finest examples of the structures serving the cult of the dead. The inside passage was high enough for a man to stand in; its walls were made by carefully fitting together nineteen great and forty smaller stone slabs. The builders tilted them slightly inward to counteract the outward thrust of the gigantic roof stones. Archaeologists have no way of estimating the tomb's capacity because it was cleaned out periodically and the accumulated bones, potsherds, and other grave offerings were ceremonially buried just outside the entrance.

The Ganges at Benares

Radio Times Hulton Picture Library

THE GREAT GODS DWELL IN RIVERS. The Ganges (Mother Ganga) is the most sacred of all the rivers in India. It is thought to issue from heaven, from the feet of the god Vishnu, and, falling on the head of the god Shiva, to drip from his hair. Pilgrims climb high in the Himalayas to pray at its glacial source. At Hardwar and Benares, steps along the banks are thronged with men and women purifying themselves in the sacred river. At Allahabad, where the Jumna flows into the Ganges, a religious fair is held; and a ritual bathing festival on an island in the Ganges Delta ushers in the new year.

In Egypt from the time of the New Empire (1580 B.C.) on, a sacred lake next to the sanctuary—as at Karnak *(left)*—was an integral part of every temple.

Fujiyama   *Viollet*

THE GREAT GODS DWELL ON MOUNTAINS. "And the Lord came down upon
mount Sinai, on the top of the mount." So it is told in the Bible. It was on
the summit of this mass of pink granite that Moses received the Ten Commandments.

Is it the grim wilderness or the thick walls built by the Emperor Justinian
(483–565) that has protected the monastery of Saint Catherine, at the foot of
Mount Sinai *(opposite)*, during its fifteen-hundred-year existence? Walls
and faith have preserved its venerable basilica, which is said to stand on the
very site where God appeared to Moses in the Burning Bush.

Opposite: Mount Sinai. *Viollet*
Overleaf, left: Mount Olympus. *Boissonnas*
Overleaf, right: Mount Everest. *Hürlimann*

**TEMPLE
CITIES**

Man had been living on earth for many thousands of years before Neolithic groups in the Middle East, not yet agriculturalists, managed the critical first steps that enabled them to domesticate most of the grains that still nourish mankind (about 6000–5000 B.C.); within a few thousand years, agriculture and stock raising had forever altered the conditions of life and the structure of society. The magnitude of the change has prompted René Girschmann to find in the Biblical account of man's expulsion from Paradise an elegy on the passing of the Neolithic Age: "The transition to the state of peasant laborer was one of the greatest revolutions in human society." With a food supply now assured, controlled, and increasing, groups crystallized into cities, each urban center distinct and self-governing, each closely tied to its surrounding lands. Even the supernatural world– the spirits and powers and godlings of nature–was affected by man's new-found power over his food supply.

It was on the plains of Mesopotamia that cities first arose. According to the Sumerian conception, a city was created to serve its god. The god owned the city, its lands and people; his house, the temple on the monumental ziggurat, was the center of the urban cluster; and in the god's service the whole community labored. Though other deities were recognized and had shrines, the city knew itself as the property of one god, and because of this belief residence, as well as kinship, came to determine a person's affinities and command his loyalties. The temple cities were thus cooperative efforts, and in their temples are found the first signs of that invention which communal organization on so considerable a scale made necessary: men invented writing to handle the affairs of the gods.

In quite another way we can read in the ruins of great mounds and temples how architecture was utilized to create the passageway for holy communication between man, insignificant and helpless, and the gods who controlled cosmic forces and manifested themselves with terrible, majestic power. In Mesopotamia, "mountain" had an emotional and religious significance as deep as that which Christians gave to the word "cross." A "mountain," according to Henri Frankfort, was where "the mysterious potency of the earth, and hence of all natural life, is concentrated," and enormous communal labor was spent to construct mountains where the flat plain offered none, manmade mountains on which the god's house could fittingly be placed. How presumptuous

Opposite: Two seated colossi, Abu Simbel. *Elisofon from* The Nile

of man to think he could lodge a god! Only the huge effort expended in creating a sacred mountain—the ziggurat, or temple tower—made men bold enough to hope that in the temple on its summit they could achieve contact with the deity.

In their gods, the citizens of the first cities expressed the pride they felt in man's creative boldness as well as the anxiety that haunted them in their new, rooted, urban way of living: the gods made it possible for man to balance courage with awareness of his utter dependence on superhuman forces. These gods, transported into different lands, transformed by very different cultures, amalgamated and developed, can be traced under different names, in myth and ritual, throughout history. Along the Nile, the Egyptians formed them into a divine host. From among the old gods, the Semites bound themselves to one in a kind of contractual relationship which the Hebrew genius later cast into the lofty ethical concept of the Palestine-born religions. Merged with the tribal gods of the early invaders of Greece, these urban gods stimulated the Athenian mind to evolve, out of this fusion and confusion, philosophical systems in which "metaphysical" was substituted for "supernatural," and an intellectual and speculative attitude replaced emotion.

Who were these gods who presided over the birth of cities and the invention of writing, these names anciently powerful and now restored to us? Erech was ruled by the god of heaven, the "pristine king and ruler," Anu. Nippur's Enlil, originally an air spirit, became the god of the land who, according to a Sumerian creation myth, broke the earth's crust with a pickax to let men sprout forth like grain; his ziggurat was significantly (if lengthily) named the "house of the Mountain, Mountain of the Storm, Bond between Heaven and Earth." Sin, the moon god, was lord of Ur; Babbar, a sun god, reigned at Larsa. Enki, enshrined at Eridu, was, as the god of sweet waters, happily pictured with fish sporting in the streams which flowed from his shoulders. Marduk, god of the Semitic city of Babylon, became the most famous, rising to greatness with his city's conquests and wealth; his priests rewrote the ancient myths of the conquered Sumerians to make Marduk the mighty hero and creator of the world and man. His ziggurat, the tower of Babylon, is remembered as the Tower of Babel. He shared his city with Ishtar, the Great Goddess (to the Greeks she was Aphrodite, the goddess of love), whose cult spread to the Mediterranean.

The Egyptians, like the Sumerians, believed that they existed to serve their god, but the god they served was incarnate in their pharaoh. To Menes they ascribed the act that gave birth to their civilization: the unification of Upper and Lower Egypt. By this he not only secured the Nile Valley against nomadic raids but also made it possible to organize an irrigation system. This is the meaning of what may be the earliest inscription (about 3200 B.C.) on a monument, which depicts a pharaoh "cutting the first sod." Thus, the institution of divine kingship provided a sense of security; for almost three thousand years Egyptian civilization maintained itself in the certain knowledge that a god had been pleased to appear among them to guide their nation and guarantee them the good will of nature's unaccountable forces and the promise of peace and prosperity.

They conceived of the afterlife as the eternal mirror of earthly life; at first it was a prerogative of the royal family; then it was extended to selected personages not of royal blood; and finally, in the cult of Osiris and even in the solar cult, it became a right all could claim. Everything in Egyptian society gravitated around the divine king: the nation's ample human and agricultural resources, her foreign trade, the genius of her artists and technicians, the labors of her priests, officials, and scribes. Everything was mobilized to insure that when, at his death, the pharaoh journeyed to rejoin the sun god, he would not lack his body, his spirit *(ba)*, or his pharaonic splendor *(ka)*.

And so we have the Pyramids, which even in ancient times commanded men's wonder, though not a trace of Memphis, the sacred city that commemorated Menes' deeds, nor of Thebes, the metropolis of the resurgent nation, nor of the palaces the living kings inhabited, has survived. It was King Zoser's architect, Imhotep, who selected Saqqara, the high ground overlooking Memphis, as the site for his master's tomb. A massive building of mud-brick faced with limestone rose in six unequal steps over the tomb to dominate the complex of buildings and courtyards needed for the mortuary ceremonies.

The Pyramid Age, after its early grandeur, diminished in architectural splendor as well as religious significance. The pyramidal cenotaph Ahmose I built at Abydos, the center of the Osiris cult, was the last one erected (c. 1800 B.C.). From then on the mortuary temples and the tombs were separated: splendid temples were built in the Nile Valley while the tombs were deep caverns secretly hollowed out from cliffs in the isolated Valley of the Kings.

In the New World the stupendous and mysterious ruins of temple cities are found from the Andean plateau, grim and treeless at thirteen thousand feet, to the humid, sea-level jungle country of Mexico. Like the people of Mesopotamia and the Nile Valley, the ancient peoples of Peru and Yucatán were innovators: they developed agricultural staples, made pottery and cloth, worked gold and silver, erected stone buildings marvelously cut and fitted and finished. They were the first to build planned cities.

We have no name for the many pre-Incaic cultures that created monuments of heroic size and bold beauty. Such is Tiahuanaco (about 500–1000 A.D.) on the Peruvian altiplano, but recently discovered. We do not know who organized and supervised its building, or who quarried and transported the heavy stone blocks, or why the huge statues of human beings were carved out of stone. Was this lonely spot the site of a tribal refuge? Did it house a priestly cult, or was it a ceremonial center to whose building many peoples contributed their labors and whose rites they shared? Was this, like Karnak, whose somber richness it resembles, a mortuary temple?

Of the Maya, more is known. Uaxactún, or nearby Tikal, is where the Maya are thought to have started building the vast centers over which the lofty temple-topped pyramids presided. From Uaxactún comes the first archaeological evidence of their religious beliefs and practices. There, a professional priesthood who had given ever-increasing importance to astronomy introduced inventions which were perfected over many centuries. Then the gods who had been identified with nature became subordinate to the impersonal workings of time; they became part of an elaborate calendar and a fantastic and accurate system of chronology. With these inventions came two others: a system of hieroglyphic writing and the corbeled roof-vaulting. These distinctive elements of the ceremonial centers were developed between 57 and 373 A.D.

Ziggurats at Eridu (*opposite*) and Ur   *Photos: Mella*

Mesopotamia

Above the Mesopotamian plains the ziggurats, mountains raised by men, still stand. They lifted the great houses built for the gods above the earth where human beings toiled to create the plenty they needed to maintain their divinities. Massive in construction, magnificently decorated, these buildings of mud-bricks were transformed into glorious shining edifices.

The temples in which the gods and goddesses dwelled are ruined. But myths and symbols which had their origins there have traveled through time and space. Thus, for example, the entwined serpent on the sacrificial goblet used by King Gudea of Lagash, about 2600 B.C., originally the emblem of the Mesopotamian god of healing, became the symbol of Asklepios, the Greek god of medicine, and is familiar to us today as the caduceus, the symbol of the medical profession.

19

Step Pyramid, Saqqara

Photos: Mella

Egypt

The Step Pyramid at Saqqara *(above)*, built about 2800 B.C., has long been dwarfed by the larger, higher, more perfectly proportioned pyramids built at Giza some three hundred years later. Yet here begins the Pyramid Age, the first of the three great building periods on the Nile. Before this the traditional method of shielding the pharaoh's burial pit was a flat superstructure, the mastaba, built out of sun-baked brick. King Zoser's architect, Imhotep, was the first to build in stone. This massive, pyramidal pile, its base 411 feet by 358 feet and its height 204 feet, dominated the underground chapels lined in blue faïence and covered with brightly colored hieroglyphs, and the templed courts. It protected the holy of holies from the elements and sought in vain to safeguard the contents of the small pink marble tomb-chamber from thieving intruders.

Of the known pyramids, none other had so rich and splendid an array of buildings constructed to cater to the pharaoh's afterlife. In the later pyramids the ritual services were symbolically enacted by paintings and carvings. Here an actual temple, a great court enclosed by a façade of dummy chapels, was built to provide the afterlife of Zoser with a proper place to re-enact his jubilee ceremony, the *heb-sed* ceremony. By the magic of this ceremony the king retained his vigor; the rite was a carry-over, it is thought, from that remote past when kings were ritually murdered in their prime lest, in their declining years, their lessening vigor cause a sympathetic lessening of the kingdom's strength.

A fascinating device of the mortuary cult are the two holes in the side of the pyramid: level with the eyes of the pharaoh's statue, they were his windows on the world.

When Chephren built his enormous pyramid and sanctuary at Giza *(right)*, about 2500 B.C., the Sphinx was already there. Carved out of solid polished rock, 240 feet long and 66 feet high, it is the Guardian of the Gates of the Underworld.

The building in the foreground is thought by some to have contained the Pavilion of the God—that is, a Purification Tent where the king's body was ritually washed, as well as a House of Embalmment where the long mummification process was carried on, and a temple where the Ceremony of the Opening of the Mouth took place—rituals which endowed the mummy with the faculties of the living. Finally, the mummy, encased in a wooden coffin to protect the now wholly divine pharaoh from human contamination, was transported along the great causeway to its secret burial place under the pyramid.

Opposite: The Sphinx and the Pyramid of Chephren, Giza

THE NEW EMPIRE (1580–1090 B.C.) was an Egypt reunited under the Theban pharaohs, liberated from the rule of the Hyksos invaders, rejuvenated and architecturally creative. A new pattern of mortuary edifice arose which, elaborated and magnified, established an ideal model that persisted until the end of the pharaonic art. Mortuary temples and tombs were a unit, even if separated one from another.

The temples of the New Empire were oriented to the morning sun. Before the pylon of each façade stood colossal statues and obelisks; above it, like a diadem, rose a mast laced with floating pennants. Next to the temple was the sacred lake or pond; the high entrance gate was approached by a sphinx-lined avenue. The portico around the inner court might have, instead of columns, a rhythmic alternation of huge pillars and statues of the mummified god Osiris. Then came a series of hypostyle halls with close-set colonnades, a thicket of eighty-foot pillars leading to the holy of holies: a chapel holding the sacred boat on which the image of the god was borne in processions, and, ultimately, in a closed, dark chamber, at the very heart of the edifice, the sacred effigy of the deity.

Egyptologists tell us that such temples, conforming to the most precise ritual observances, were conceived of as an "image of the universe." The pylon was the symbol of the goddesses Isis and Nephthys, between whom the sun—the obelisk—rested in its course. The decoration of walls and columns represented the dense vegetation of palm trees, lotus, and papyrus upholding the heavens—a ceiling scattered with stars, and lintels carved with the image of the sun. The presence of Isis and Nephthys and the statues of the mummified Osiris reveal that the ancient worship of Amon-Ra, the sun god, had accepted the added reassurance promised by the Osiris cult.

Osiris, the greatest of the gods of ancient Egypt, has been described by Henri Frankfort as the "god-man who suffered, died, was buried, rose again from the dead, and entered into heaven where he reigns eternally." As King of the Otherworld, Osiris stood with forty-two assessors in the Judgment Hall to which the dead were immediately brought and judged. Those who were found worthy lived in the Osirian paradise in eternal bliss. To be worthy, the dead had to be magically identified with Osiris, by formulas, amulets, and observance of the embalming process as related in his myth.

Mortuary temple, Thebes   *Mella*

The mortuary temple of the Eighteenth Dynasty shown at left was built at the beginning of the New Empire as part of the city of the dead. It stands on the bank of the Nile opposite the Thebes of the "living god." The pharaohs of this dynasty chose to be buried in the desert; in the rocky Valley of Kings, archaeologists have found the vast Theban necropolis.

The Great Temple of Amon-Ra, Karnak *Viollet*

At Karnak, between solemn sphinxes, an avenue led to the quay *(in the foreground above)* where the sacred boat was moored. The sphinxes have the heads of rams, the animal of Amon-Ra. The statue of Rameses II, who built the great temple in 1250 B.C., is in the holy form of the mummified Osiris – evidence that the Osiris cult had become part of the ancient sun worship.

The monumental hypostyle hall of Karnak is the most impressive of Egyptian sacred edifices. Built during the reign of three great pharaohs, it is vast enough to contain the whole of Notre Dame. Its towering columns constitute a veritable forest of light and shade, the sunlight of Amon-Ra and the everlasting gloom of the Underworld. The columned central nave rose 33 feet above the thickset columns of the many-sided aisles. When the ceilings were intact, the capitals of the central avenue – papyrus plants in full flower – were lighted by clerestory openings and contrasted sharply with the shadowed side columns topped with capitals of papyrus buds. Indeed, the massive columns placed close together gave the illusion of a solid stone tomb, while the animation of the brightly painted carvings spoke of the certainty of resurgent life.

23

As Karnak was the residence of Amon-Ra, so Luxor *(right)* was the temple where the god was feted and entertained. An avenue, two miles long and flanked by ram-headed sphinxes, connected the two sanctuaries. Annually, Amon-Ra went to his pleasure-palace accompanied by a great retinue of other gods, each in his own golden sacred boat glittering with precious stones, carried on large floats on the Nile from temple to temple. Singers and dancers along the shore accompanied the procession.

Luxor was built on ground already holy—so an earlier sanctuary reveals. And its sanctity outlived the rites of Amon-Ra. Here under the Ptolemies in Hellenistic times was a Roman-style shrine to Isis, goddess of the Serapis cult; here Coptic Christian churches were built on the temple's east side, a short while before Moslems erected a mosque in the midst of the Egyptian pillars. The alien minarets look down on deserted temples.

Abu Simbel *(see page $\overline{14}$)*, one of the two great sanctuaries Rameses II sculptured out of the lofty cliff, was dedicated to Harmakhis, an ancient local godling associated with Horus, son of Osiris and Isis. Horus was the infant morning-sun, represented as a falcon or a falcon-headed man wearing the solar disk.

The god's statue stands in the central niche over the entrance. Above him, dwarfed in size, is a frieze of dog-headed figures standing to salute the sun, whose first rays shine on them. Below, between the legs of the seated statues—63 feet high—are queens and princesses; under their pedestals are small statues of falcon-headed Horus, and Osiris in mummified form.

Rock-hewn sanctuaries, sculptured from mighty cliffs, were created in many parts of the world influenced by Egypt. The Persians carried the idea and technique eastward to India, where other temple masterpieces, honoring other gods, were carved. It went up the Nile to Ethiopia, where the great Christian churches of Lalibela were carved in medieval times.

From ancient times Hathor, the cow-headed goddess, was worshiped in the temple shown below. Once a year she went up the Nile to Idfu. Hathor's name means "house of Horus," and she was associated with that divinity. But, like other great goddesses such as Ishtar and Cybele, she had many functions. She was the goddess of love and the protectress of the dead in their desert cemeteries; in time she became the divine model of womanhood.

Mella

Temple of Hathor, Dendera

Temple of Amon, Luxor. *Elisofon from* The Nile

Isis and the infant Horus

The triad of Osiris, Isis, and Horus, whose cultic center was Abydos, was a favorite theme for Egyptian sculptors. The figure of Isis suckling the infant Horus was adapted by Egyptian Christians to depict the Madonna and the infant Jesus in the same tender motif.

Metropolitan Museum of Art: Rogers Fund 1945

25

Pyramid of the Sun, Teotihuacán.

The Americas

In the New World are majestic ceremonial centers. Teotihuacán, a Nahuatl word meaning "The Home of the Gods," proclaims the celestial as Versailles speaks of the regal and New Delhi of the imperial. Started at the beginning of the Christian era, it was the greatest and most influential of Mesoamerica's ceremonial centers. Though Teotihuacán was sacked and burnt by invaders about A. D. 650, its form served as the model for all succeeding empires—the Toltec, the Aztec and the Spanish—in the Valley of Mexico.

Teotihuacán is vast and impressive. An area three and a half miles long by two miles wide—an area paved and repaved with plaster—is covered with temples and houses for the priestly community. Of the many enormous buildings within this sacred area, the Pyramid of the Sun is the largest: a truncated pile mounting in four great terraces to a height of two hundred feet. The slopes of the several terraces were cunningly varied by their builders to increase the overwhelming feeling of massiveness, and their exterior surfaces were faced with stone and finished with smooth plaster.

Monumental structures, such as the Temple of Quetzalcoatl *(opposite)*, the Feathered Serpent and god of learning, were built of rubble behind the stone facing. Originally the sculptured images were painted in fierce colors, and the Feathered Serpent glared through brightly polished obsidian eyes.

The Aztecs, a militaristic people whose bloodthirsty rituals promoted warfare, built on the Toltec beginnings. The Aztecs' temples are known to us from codices, texts, and a few excavated sites. Both their religious architecture and their gods were taken over from the Toltecs.

Temple of Quetzalcoatl. *Photos: Viollet*

Monte Albán, Oaxaca   *Viollet*

In addition to the Toltec and Aztec civilizations of Mexico, there were other cultures, in other regions, having other languages, gods, and religious architecture. At Monte Albán, the magnificent ceremonial center of the Zapotecs at Oaxaca *(left)*, the summit of a small mountain was leveled off and terraced to form a platform high above the valley. Under the influence of the Toltecs, Monte Albán assumed a grandiose spatial arrangement while it preserved its own regional theology and decorative language.

Mixtec temple Mitla   *Paul Popper Ltd.*

Late in the development of the Zapotecs, another people, the Mixtecs, migrated into the Valley of Oaxaca. Their exquisite temples at Mitla *(left)* are utterly different from the nearby Zapotec ceremonial center. The Mixtecs carried the art of mosaic work into architecture. Their low-lying, corridored temples have a marvelous and intricate veneer of stones cut to form a patterned surface.

Mayan temple, Uxmal   *Viollet*

Though we have found dozens of the huge white ceremonial centers erected by the Mayas in Yucatán, which seem to float above the enveloping bush, and though we can appreciate the elegant Mayan art, read their hieroglyphic numerals, admire their intellectual achievements, and trace their far-flung trade, we are not even certain what this people called itself. The Mayan temples, varied in form and decoration, lifted high on massive piles of stone, as at Uxmal *(left)*, have a few tiny rooms to which the priests alone had access.

Chichén Itzá   *Viollet*

Of the many Mayan temples, only Chichén Itzá *(above)*, ruled after its political decline
by the Aztecs, who extended their empire over the Mayans, is similar to the spacious
ceremonial centers built in the Valley of Mexico. These monumental religious architectural achievements and the slight traces of humble secular life remind us of Valliant's
comment on the magnitude of "the toll which men exact from themselves for their
salvation."

We know less of pre-Columbian Peru, one of the South American cultures best known to us, than we do of the high civilizations of Mesopotamia and Egypt. Our knowledge is as pathetically fragmentary as our datings are uncertain. More and more we are beginning to appreciate the many independent and unique cultures which preceded the Incaic empire, the only culture commonly thought to cover the entire story of pre-conquest Peru. So, for example, archaeologists have found that the Chavín horizon–a religious cult embracing a wide area with different societies, tentatively dated from 850 to 500 B.C.–had a fully developed complex of plazas and ceremonial platforms, terraces and mounds as shown below; these elements were subsequently employed in sacred architecture. At that early date and with no prior experimentation, there was an accomplished mastery of stone construction.

Tiahuanaco belongs to what has been called the "Expansionist Period," when some sort of political power carried with it the Tiahuanaco cult. Shrouded in mystery, impressive in appearance, it has invited wild speculation–it has even been claimed as the place where civilization itself had its birth. The principal structures–four major ones and several minor ones–cover a sixth of a square mile; built entirely of stone, each carefully carved, these great lines of megalithic monuments are among the world's finest masonry. The most famous is the mighty "Gateway of the Sun," carved out of a single block, ten feet high, twelve and a half feet wide, and weighing about ten tons. The vast site was never finished; work on it stopped while it was still incomplete.

The drawing at left, depicting the dedication of the Great Temple, or *Cu*, of Mexico, is from the *Codex Telleriano*, one of the few surviving Aztec books. An entry in the annals for the year "Eight Canes" (1487), the picture indicates that twenty thousand men from provinces which the Aztecs had subjugated by war were slain at the dedication ceremony.

Great Serpent effigy mound, southern Ohio   *Smithsonian Institution*

About a thousand years ago the Indians in the midwestern United States built their extraordinary "effigy mounds," huge figures of animals or birds made of raised earth. It is thought that the serpentine figure above, thirteen hundred feet of curving length and about a yard high, had some connection with a tribal religious organization. Certainly, none of the men who labored to form this effigy could ever have seen their work as clearly as it appears in this aerial view.

31

This unusual drawing was made by a Spaniard traveling aboard the first European ship to touch at Nootka Sound, off Vancouver Island, in 1727. In the shrine he pictured, probably set up near the Indian medicine man's house, is the ageless spirit, summoned from the depths of the water to do its master's bidding.

Nootka shrine,
Vancouver Island

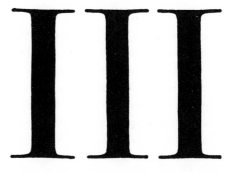

**HINDUISM,
BUDDHISM,
AND
JAINISM**

India has been called the most religious of nations. Her religious climate has made her civilization influential, distinctive, and recognizable. The land bears witness to her spiritual zeal—temples and ruins of temples are everywhere. They encompass an enormous range of religious beliefs: from popular forms of magic and animism, to a pious and orthodox personal faith, to a highly developed system of meditation and speculation concerned with the meaning of God and nature, man and his role in the universe.

Her spiritual languages, whether Buddhist, Jainist, Hindu, or Brahman, center on spiritual freedom. Nonattachment is the goal sought. Those who suffer in this world hope by freeing themselves from consciousness of self to attain the blissful peace of the impersonal world mind—the names vary according to the language.

Because each man must find his own way to escape this world, Indian temples—except for the chapels which served the Buddhist monastic communities—no matter how vast in size, are less halls of worship as we understand them than they are sacred monuments, each a tabernacle enclosing the divine image in a space of "superluminous darkness." In a man-made twilight, before an altar of the shining ones, the worshiper pursues his search for liberation—repeats and repeats his soundless cry: "Lead me from the unreal to the Real; lead me from darkness to Light; lead me from death-in-life to Immortality."

Indian religions stress that each man discovers his own key to spiritual freedom in his own spiritual resources—a metaphysical task that has inspired the practices of yoga. Yoga is not worship but a technique—meditation is part of it—by which a person may achieve emancipation from cosmic laws through physical, mental, and emotional discipline. This practice and belief are indigenous. Archaeologists have dug out of long-buried cities of the Indus Valley civilization (c. 2500 B.C.) steatite seals on which are engraved a god in the position of a yogi. Sitting with legs bent double, heel-to-heel, in a posture a body would not normally assume, he is the prototype of yoga practices and later religious sculpture.

The attributes of this earliest male god—he is horned, three-faced, and surrounded by an elephant, a tiger, a rhinoceros, and a buffalo—become those of the later great Hindu god Shiva, Lord of Beasts and Prince of Yogis. Similarly, the deer close to the god's throne anticipate the sculptured scenes of the Buddha preaching the Deer Park Sermon. Other pre-Aryan seals add elements still holy, still venerated: the sun, the phallus and navel-stone, the sacred fig tree (pipal), snakes, and the hump-backed bull, still respectfully permitted to wander at will. The quantities of clay female figurines placed on those ancient household altars are like the votive offerings found today on rural shrines. In one form they represent the Mother Goddess; in another, identified by her skull-like features, grim and grinning, she is the deity of the underworld into whose awful power both the seed and the corpse buried in the earth are committed.

Stability of symbols is one aspect of Indian religions and temples. But of equal significance are the historical development, the new meanings and emphases given such symbols. Knowledge of the Vedic period (3000–1500 B.C.), which followed the Aryan invasions, comes from the Rig Veda, a massive collection of prayers, hymns, and incantations compiled in the eleventh and twelfth centuries B.C. The Aryan conquerors had no temples: the domestic hearth sufficed, or, if an animal was to be sacrificed, they tethered it to the sacrificial post *(yupa)* next to a simple altar of dried turf. (They used brick after they learned the art of brick-making from the conquered people.) Hymns and rituals were largely concerned with the events of everyday living (plowing the fields or driving the cattle to new pastures) and, if chants and gestures had been correctly followed, the priest could calmly remind the god, "We have our wishes, you have our gifts."

By the seventh and eighth centuries B.C., this primitive give-and-get religion no longer satisfied deeper spiritual needs; these had developed a body of priestly liturgical exegesis of the Vedic books. The Brahmanas (hence Brahmanism) and the Upanishads were excursions into philosophical and metaphysical problems—whence we are born, what kind of world we live in, and whither we go. These theological works suggest that the period of Aryanization was succeeded by one of amalgamation with the earlier religious ideas of the conquered. Much of the doctrine of the Upanishads was of Kshatriya (warrior caste) origin; yet in this process of amalgamation the position of the priests (the Brahmins) was strengthened; they had the importance formerly held by the warrior caste.

It was in revolt against such a priest-dominated religion that Buddhism and Jainism arose. Prince Siddhartha (c. 563–483 B.C.) of the royal house of Gautama, known and revered as the Buddha (from the Sanskrit: "The Enlightened One"), and his older contemporary Vardhamana, called Mahavira, "The Great Hero," and Jina, "The Victor" (c. 599–527 B.C.), both in their spiritual goals and in the way of life they taught, seem to Western minds brothers to the great prophets of the Old Testament; the ethics of Buddhism and Jainism have profound similarities to those of the major Western religions. Both teachers also introduced, each in his own way, new interpretations of two basic Indian concepts: that of reincarnation—that all sentient beings were bound to the wheel of rebirth—and that of karma—that they were so bound by the necessary consequences of their actions. Against an orthodoxy which accepted the possibility of escape from these forces but offered no clear reasons, Buddhism and Jainism taught how—and why—people *can* escape the pull of this "gravitational field" and enter another from which there is no rebirth because karma no longer binds. After practicing ascetic austerities and long meditation, both Gautama and Vardhamana experienced their blessed triumphs. Each one attracted disciples and inspired men to follow his example.

The spread of Buddhism and Jainism introduced new images, symbols, and meanings into the mainstream of Indian religion and religious art. The "air-clothed" Jain ascetic provided the prototype for the all-but-naked statues of the Jain saints and the Buddhas and also for the face, unrelentingly severe, expressionless, stripped of all emotion, which, carved in stone, confronts us.

Buddhism's contributions were fundamental and its influences richer, greater, and more lasting than those of Jainism. Its long tenure began when the Emperor Ashoka (273–232 B. C.) made Buddhism the state religion. As such it enjoyed the royal patronage and – of equal importance to religious architecture – mobilized the skill of artisans who, using familiar building themes and ancient magical motifs to tell the story of the Buddha, imparted to their task their new-found spiritual joy. The sacred monuments built with imperial largesse, from Ashoka's conversion to about 600 A. D., served as models for the construction of temples to house the Hindu gods when Brahmanism replaced Buddhism as the official religion; and also furnished patterns for Buddhist sculpture and architecture outside India.

Of the Buddhist monuments constructed during those centuries, comparatively few have survived: a handful of monolithic pillars, the archaeological debris of brick and wood edifices, a fraction of the impressive stupas raised over relics or to commemorate sacred sites, and scattered rock-cut chapels and monasteries. Yet we know the land was filled with renowned religious centers, for they were visited and glowingly described by Chinese pilgrims. Most of these early Buddhist structures lay in the murderous path cut across northern India by the White Huns (c. 450 A. D.), who, it is estimated, razed sixteen hundred stupas, chapels, and university clusters.

From the rock-cut chapels and monasteries established in remote valleys a record of development of more than a thousand years, from the third century B. C. to the eighth century A. D., has been pieced together. There we can read how the Buddhist creed was profoundly altered – actually see the differences between the early phase, Hinayana Buddhism, when the Buddha was the great Teacher (in India this phase ended soon after the start of our era), and the subsequent, Mahayana phase of Buddhism, when the Buddha had been elevated to divinity. In the Hinayana chapels, the Buddha's image never appeared: he is always represented by symbols, imaginative and artless, and by scenes of his life, his experiences, and his teachings. The Mahayana chapels present a sharp contrast. A luxuriance of Buddha images reflects the new belief in a multiplicity of Buddhas, among them Sakyamuni Buddha himself, the founder of the faith and now a personal savior; Maitreya, the future Buddha of the present world-cycle; and finally Amitabha Buddha, the gracious Ruler of the Western Paradise. The definite promises of Mahayana Buddhism and its capacity to absorb the myriad of celestials who, as Bodhisattvas, surrounded and served the Buddha, made it welcome wherever it was carried.

Buddhism, which had become so accommodating to ancient gods and goddesses and their symbolic animals, became in its popular forms almost indistinguishable from Hinduism with its throng of deities, its rituals and ceremonies, and its powerful priestly class. With scarcely a sigh it yielded its primacy in India to the older religion. Hinduism, which in its turn had incorporated some of the teachings and practices of the ascetics, became established as the state religion.

WATER AND SACRED IMAGES have always played an important part in the religions of India. Water is life-giving; it has
holy properties; holy water washes away mortal suffering,
sin, and evil. If a temple is not near a river, a pond, or the sea,
an artificial pool will serve. So will a simple jar of water placed
at the shrine's entrance. The Great Bath located at the heart
of Mohenjo-Daro, a prehistoric city of the Indus Valley,
attests the antiquity of this belief. It anticipates the sacred
bathing places along the Ganges, always crowded with pilgrims, as well as the superb water architecture, designed,
as at Modhera *(opposite)*, as an integral part of an impressive
temple complex.

Figure from a Bhuvanesvara temple, eleventh century
  Tank in the Great Temple at Modhera, seventeenth century

36

Basic motifs were woven into Hindu cosmology—snakes, for example, whose holiness was ancient and special. The broad expanded hoods of the mighty serpent, Shesha, support the earth and heavens, and in the security of his mighty coils the god Vishnu, Preserver and Supporter of the Universe, often reclines and rests *(left)*. Snakes indicate underground water, on which creation and procreation depend; water is the "first tangible emanation" of Vishnu's divine essence.

Vishnu resting on Shesha   *Hürlimann*

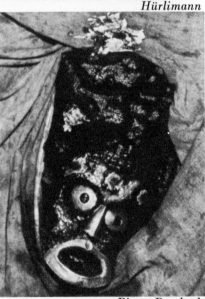

Durga

Pierre Rambach

Female figurines represent both the benevolent Mother of the Universe, the auspicious Earth Goddess, the Goddess of Fertility and Prosperity, and the wrathful, terrible, and prodigious Durga *(left)*, also known as Kali, the Dark One who relentlessly swallows mankind. The sexual ringstone or *yoni*, a circle hollowed out in the center, symbolizes the female principle, worshiped in conjunction with the stone phallus or *lingam*, symbol of the originally nameless god. The act of love and the *lingam–yoni*, a stone block set on a round stone base, have the same meaning; again and again the embrace between the cosmic male and female, *maithuna*, is realistically depicted on Hindu temples to give form to the metaphysical idea of the primordial union of pairs of opposites.

Ring-stones found at
Mohenjo-Daro,
Indus Valley

Statue of Shiva at Elephanta

Shiva dances: South Indian figure

Shiva himself resembles the three-faced divinity carved on an Indus Valley seal in the yoga position. A magnificent eighth-century statue in a rock-cut cave-temple at Elephanta *(above)* isolates the traits in this triune image: the face on the right shows him as Creator, that on the left as Destroyer, while his central aspect, "irradiated," as Dr. Kramrisch says, "by the realization of the Absolute," wears a crown shaped like the *lingam* which is enshrined in Shiva's sanctuaries.

At other times Shiva is known as Lord of the Dance, Nataraja. The statuette *(right)* expresses the myth: the god dancing the dance of creation, existence, and annihilation. While extinguishing the world, the god by his very movements becomes the source of life.

Carving on a Jain temple on Mount Girnar, thirteenth century   *Viollet*

Sacred Architecture in India

The ultimate goal of religion is spiritual liberation, the individual's release from the travail of birth and rebirth, to attain, finally, reintegration in the Absolute. Buddhism, Jainism, and Hinduism mapped the physical, psychological, and metaphysical requirements to be fulfilled in the worshiper's own body, a body which had been severely disciplined, rigorously controlled, and patiently readied.

The rich mural ornamentation—painting and sculpture, as on the temples illustrated—is thought of as the divine counterpart of ideal human beauty fittingly adorned. Temples and shrines are meant to be looked at, and their decoration to facilitate meditation. Sculpture served theology, proclaiming the great power of the gods, "their causal bodies and active presence." The divinities and their celestial attendants on the walls became actors in the sacred drama played in the theater of the worshiper's heart; the sculpture was intended to awaken, inspire, inform, and fortify the worshiper for contemplation – not, as has been thought, for idolatry.

The extraordinary plastic sense of the Indian sculptors was the product of a systematic training. Because the temples required scores of skilled artisans, they were recruited from many parts of the land, and such men moved about with their families and household goods; they remained with their children and, if need be, their children's children, until the building was finished. From father to son, the skills and styles were inculcated, work and instruction starting at childhood. Practice and theory were unified; technical lore transmitted orally accompanied each stage of the teaching. This workshop language, codified and ritualized by the priests, was incorporated into treatises from which the workman learned the language of his art. Using such treatises, the artisan skillfully carried out the religion's aesthetic and theological aim. His work was sacred, for through his images the god poured out divine power.

40

Left: Sculptured surface, South Gate of the Great Temple at Madura

The idioms of Buddhist and Hindu sculpture differ. The images of the Buddha have been called variations on the theme of silence. Images of Hindu gods, on the other hand, are divinities caught in the fullest moment of their holy power, charging the myth with the cosmic significance of their actions.

The Westerner confronted with so strange a spiritual landscape can find Indian temples too big and too much. Stupendous ornamentation crowding vast surfaces—a frenzied foam of images whose meaning is unknown, alien, or (for some) obscene—can leave the Westerner astonished, fatigued, and (often) aghast.

Hindu temples have been divided into two major architectural styles: the Northern, or Indo-Aryan, and the Southern, or Dravidian. The differences are neither religious nor regional. Both housed the same gods and utilized the same sacrosanct themes, and the styles are often juxtaposed in the same locality. Temples have also been classified according to the dynasties which, in the familiar rhythm of vigorous rise, conquest, power, and decline, glorified their rule with temple building. Only a few remain.

The Great Temple, Madura   *Photos: Paul Popper Ltd.*

THE UNITS that compose Buddhist and Hindu sacred monuments repeat architectural themes found as far away as the Near East and the Mediterranean and as long ago as the time of the megalithic cults. There are six such units—(1) the enclosure, (2) the gate, (3) the altar, (4) the mountain, (5) the pillar, and (6) the cave.

The *enclosure*, as at Rameswaram *(below)*, separates sacred space from secular space. It also insures that as the worshiper performs the rites of circumambulation the shrine's holy emanations will clothe him. The enclosure can be formed by a railing, a wall, or a passageway and can be repeated to create a series of ambulatories, arranged either concentrically or in tiers. The Buddhist cave-chapels had aisles between the walls and interior columns to serve as ambulatories. In the temples housing Hindu gods, the enclosures might be pillared galleries or closed passages within the structure itself.

A pillared passageway, Rameswaram, seventeenth century

Hürlimann

The *gate* form, *torana*, is most famous far from the place of its origin. Its form, distinctive and memorable, traveled with Buddhism to the Far East. It is the *piu-lu* of China and the familiar *torii* of Japan, where it is used almost as a signature for a temple.

The Great Stupa at Sanchi, built in the middle of the second century B.C., has four gates leading to the shrine. They are richly carved with symbol and image. We know from an inscription that the North Gate *(opposite)* was sculpted by ivory carvers. Its message, the story of the Buddha's life and experiences depicted in intensely moving imagery, prepared the worshiper to find the answer to his anguish in the Path taught by the Buddha.

The gate, or more properly, the approach-structure, to the Hindu temple has a different function and development. The earliest shrines had a single door prefaced by a shallow porch. Hindu temples still have one doorway, the only approach to the "holy of holies." As rituals and ceremonies became more elaborate, galleries, vestibules, halls, pavilions, and balconies were added, all leading to this single doorway.

Opposite: North Gate, Sanchi

The Great Stupa, Sanchi *Viollet*

The *altar* and the *mountain* are closely related. The altar on which the priests lighted the sacrificial fire was the earliest sacred construction. Built for Vedic rites, it was a horizontal mass of bricks piled up to represent the mythical Mount Meru located somewhere north of the Himalayas. Mount Meru, sacred to the pre-Aryan peoples, became the World Mountain on whose summit the Aryan gods had their celestial mansions. It represented both the central mountain of the universe, making the midpoint of the earth's surface, and the vertical axis of the egg-shaped cosmos. This dual significance determined the meaning also given to the Buddhist stupas. Within the enclosure and gate was the sixteen-foot terrace, the altar-mountain; on it the spherical mound, the egg, *anda*. Together they symbolized Nirvana, the transcendent reality beyond forms. The plain hemisphere built of solid brick with a masonry covering was fifty-four feet high, and above it rose the finial in the shape of a tiered umbrella, the sign of royalty.

Stupas originated as cairns raised over hallowed relics. Altar and sphere inspired monumental variations: stupa and terrace grew in height and number, repeated and elaborated. As with an offering perpetually renewed, this repetition increased and intensified the emotional impact of the original motifs.

The Hindus also placed their temples, such as the Kesava temple at Somnathpur *(below)* on altar-terraces. When Hinduism became the dominant faith and temples for Hindu gods were built, they too duplicated the same unit—terrace and shrine, terrace and shrine, diminishing in size as it ascended—to form their towered sanctuaries.

Kesava temple at Somnathpur, built in 1268

Right: One of the Ashoka pillars
at Mauriya Nandangarh,
in Bihar

Far right: Free-standing pillar in
the Kailasa temple, Ellora,
c. 700 A.D.

The famous *pillars* erected in the third century B.C. by King Ashoka after his conversion to Buddhism appear to have been placed on sites hallowed by the Buddha: they guided pilgrims along a way of holy places. Of the thirty-odd original ones, only two are standing where they were planted. Each pillar is a forty-foot shaft of polished sandstone, with a sacred symbol rising another ten feet. Two feet in diameter at the top, each is hewn from a single stone. The pillars suggest the archaic function of holding the firmament high to provide an ordered space between earth and sky wherein man could move. Today poles festooned with flags and streamers stand in the enclosure of Hindu temples.

At some time the Indian genius for metaphysical thought gave the pillar a symbolic dimension: it had a spatial position but no magnitude. The Buddhists, as in the Great Stupa at Sanchi, thought of the pillar as being encased in the spherical mound; the finial showed where the pillar ended to provide the pedestal for the honorific umbrella. A symbolic pillar was the central theme for Hindu temples which embody the cosmic myth of existence. Thus the spire or tower of a Shiva temple symbolized divine creative activity, as the *lingam*, Shiva's cult image, represented the actual state of procreativeness. The inner "pillar"—transmuted into a "more-imaginary-than-real" shaft—was clothed in the mountain-like masonry of the soaring spire; it was conceived as starting from the ground, passing through the image of the temple's small sanctuary, rising on up through the solid tower to pierce the ring-stone. Above, on the very top of the "pillar," was the finial toward which the pillar pointed and toward which the swelling monumental mass reached. The finial, simple and supreme, gathered in structure and sculpture: it was the manifestation of the moment of Release. (The finial of a Hindu temple dedicated to Shiva is a trident; that of a temple to Vishnu is a disk or wheel.)

The *cave* is a continually repeated Indian architectural theme. It is a small cavity whose name means the "womb-house," or the "germ-cell," which holds the sacred image. Windowless, a twilight darkness encloses the ultimate mystery. The temple's exterior can be studied by visitors as well as worshipers but the former are not permitted to view the "holy of holies." Through the single door, which usually faces east, the rays of the early-morning sun reach straight into the sanctum to permit the god's entry into his earthly house and the daily renewal of his glory. Through this same door the worshiper gazes on the holy image and meditates or prays, perhaps for a favorable rebirth. The location of the "womb-house" deep within the solid masonry of the temple, and its dim quiet in which, it seems, time itself is swallowed up, give the sanctuary the quality of a cave and suggest the sanctity accorded certain caves in India.

THE BUDDHIST ROCK-CUT CHAPELS might be thought of as man-made caves. Such architecture first reached India in the second century B.C.

Near Bombay is Karli *(below, left)*, one of the finest of the cave-chapels, aesthetically satisfying and emotionally moving, a classroom where living pupils could listen undistracted to their great Teacher. Only the stupa, an undisguised gravemound, severe in its plainness, clearly spoke of the ultimate release from the pains and precariousness of existence. The chapel, 124 feet long, 46 feet wide, and 45 feet high, was entered through three doorways; the central one, for priests and royalty, had a ramp flanked by shallow pools through which the worshipers waded to wash away worldly contamination.

The Buddhist cave-chapel was a large vaulted hall divided longitudinally by two rows of columns to form a wide nave with side aisles and an apsidal end for the enshrined stupa-image. Similar to the basilica then being evolved in Europe, the chapel was a commodious assembly hall. The nave held the congregation while the side aisles, continuing around the apsidal end, were the ambulatories for circumambulating the stupa. The huge horseshoe archway placed above the doorway at Bhaja *(below, right)* was the sun-window; through it the light was brought to rest on the holy stupa.

Karli cave-chapel, c. 50 B.C.   *Hürlimann*

Caves at Ajanta, 150 B.C.–642 A.D.   *Mella*

The cave-chapels were inspired edifices. Conjured out of solid rock, they stand now, empty, deserted, silent, having survived the destructions wrought by time and man. In the Hinayana chapels, the Buddha, not yet a god nor yet carved in the likeness of man, was represented symbolically—by his throne, his footprint (see page 62), his umbrella—to remind his followers of his life and teachings.

At Ajanta, shown above, where a vertical cliff curves with the river running in the valley below, twenty-eight façades show how large was the monastic population which carved cells, assembly halls, and chapels in that remote valley. The work started around 150 B.C. Suddenly in 642 A.D. the work stopped. The country was conquered. Tools thrown down by the workmen tell us of their fear and flight. In all, some twelve hundred chapels large and small are scattered in suitable terrain throughout India. Only in the mid-seventh century, when the art of building in masonry had been perfected and temples could be located wherever the royal patron desired, did this kind of architectural sculpture end. During the centuries when it was practiced, India created sacred monuments unequaled in any other land.

Left: Exterior of chapel, Bhaja caves, second century B.C.

47

Gandharan figure of Buddha, first century A.D.

Buddhas

When Mahayana Buddhism arose, "art awakened with an archaic smile from a past of symbols and legends." Now, as it were, the ancient minor gods and spirits, reformed by the Buddha's spiritual innovations, reappear in a new guise as Bodhisattvas, compassionate saviors beyond the dualism of "world" and Nirvana, who have paradoxically refused final Nirvana for themselves, until all beings can enter with them. These superhuman answers to men's needs surround the godlike Buddha as their Hindu visual equivalents attend Shiva or Vishnu.

Gandhara was a place: its name signifies Greco-Roman-Buddhist art. Gandharan artisans, by inventing the Buddha image, made a lasting contribution to the art of Asia. Diverse aesthetic styles flowed into that northwestern part of India where the Buddha, given human form, was made accessible. Here the Kushan empire flourished, maintaining ties with Rome, whose deified emperors, carved as gods, were enshrined in temples. The earliest Buddha statues are hardly distinguishable from an Apollo Belvedere draped in a toga of imperial Rome.

Gandharan Bodhisattva

Seated Buddha, Taxila

Right: Buddha from cave 19,
Ajanta, sixth century A.D.

Opposite: Buddha, Sarnath

In the early Mahayana cave-chapel at Ajanta shown below, the Buddha images, set in niches and panels, portray the radiance and grace of the god's Nirvana-won wisdom: they surround and support the worshiper. Everywhere amiable spirits fly with heavenly energy and joy. Truly Mahayana Buddhism was the "Great Vehicle" which would carry to bliss–ultimately, Buddhahood–all who invoked the compassion of the Buddha and Bodhisattvas by offerings and prayers. The stupa no longer seems a mere gravemound. The rock has become transparent, and we seem to be able to look into the mound to the pillared, canopied niche where the Buddha stands in spiritual serenity.

Mahayana cave-chapel, Ajanta   *Hürlimann*

Kailasa temple, Ellora

Ellora

The Hindu temple Kailasa, Shiva's paradise, at Ellora, has been called the most stupendous single work of art executed in India. To say this, to explain that it is a mountainside carved to look like a building–the Kailasa covers an area similar to that of the Parthenon in Athens and is half again as high–does nothing to convey the mystery and poetry of the temple. Each part of the enormous complex of shrines is a work of art, gracefully proportioned and admirably related to the whole. This image of Shiva's paradise–Mount Kailasa in the Himalayas, where the god and his eternally lovely bride,

Parvati, celebrate their sacred union—is dedicated to their act of love, the source and guarantee of cosmic harmony. The temple was begun under the patronage of King Krishna I, 757–783; for the next two hundred years his successors committed their unlimited resources to its completion.

The first operation outlined the temple's perimeter by huge trenches cut into the mountainside that isolated a mass of solid stone 276 feet long, 154 feet wide, and, at its apex, 100 feet high. All rock-cut architecture is worked from the top down; it obviates the need for scaffolding—excavating such a monument involves less labor than building it would. First the rock-cutters roughed out the contours, and immediately behind them came the sculptors, carving, refining, smoothing. Step by step, by planning and coordination, the work progressed downward until the courtyard was reached and the glorious temple, freed from the mountain, stood formed and finished.

Ellora gives us tolerance sanctioned by religion. There thirty-four temples in all, housing Buddhist, Hindu, and Jain gods, stand side by side. "To show bigotry toward other faiths," wrote the wise Shivaji, "is to tamper with God's work, for He manifests Himself in multifarious ways to different peoples." At Ellora, priests, architects, and master craftsmen created a series of mammoth sculptured sanctuaries. Blow by blow, thousands of hammers and chisels—each little more than a quarter of an inch wide—nibbled at the hills to reveal the eternal gods of India.

Mahabalipuram

From Mahabalipuram, near Madras, once the busy seaport of the Pallava Dynasty, trading ships sailed regularly to Java and Cambodia. The town was the gateway through which Buddhism and Hinduism were spread to the islands of the Indian Ocean; the missionaries who sailed from it took with them not only their holy messages but the Pallava style of religious architecture and sculpture. Today it is a waste of sand dunes strewn with extraordinary mementos of its past glory. Its only inhabitants, a bull, an elephant, a lion, and monkeys, are as rooted as the indestructible granite rocks from which they were carved.

The anonymous Pallava sculptors rank among the world's finest artists. In the remarkable allegory of the descent of the Ganges, created when their king was converted from Buddhism to Hinduism, about 600 to 625, the artists sought to fix forever that moment when the celestial Ganges miraculously descended from heaven. To the left of a vertical cleft in the rock (not shown) they depicted the ordeals suffered by gods, human beings, and animals. On the other side (opposite), we see the jubilant creatures of the earth led by elephants hastening to behold and worship. Above them rush fast-moving spirits and floating divinities. Between supplication and hosanna is the prodigious event itself: the serpent god, or naga, symbol of life-giving water, rises triumphantly from his underground domain. Traces of an irrigation system show that water from the nearby Palar River was brought to the rock to provide a jeweled waterfall curtain through which the water spirits happily swam upward.

Opposite: The Descent of the Ganges; part of the frieze of Arjuna's Penance, 88 feet long and 30 feet high, at Mahabalipuram

Bodhnath stupa, Katmandu *Hürlimann*

NEPAL received religious and graphic influences from near and far. From India came the massive stupa and the soaring tower, from Afghanistan the colossal size and frontality of holy images, from Tibet a stylized mystical symbolism, and from distant China the pagoda. The Newars of Nepal adapted what they wanted to their own aesthetics and religious cults.

The two-thousand-year-old Bodhnath *(left)*, still revered though Buddhism has almost disappeared from Nepal, is one of the two stupas which remained intact where Ashoka planted them. For it was the emperor himself who went as a pilgrim to Nepal and erected countless stupas to celebrate his success in converting the valley's inhabitants. At some later time, above the original Sanchi-type stupa a tall thirteen-tiered spire was added, and on each side of its base are painted two large half-open eyes, whose mesmerizing gaze watches over the high valley in which Katmandu is set.

JAIN doctrine teaches that the founder Vardhamana was the last in a succession of twenty-four teachers. All have become superhuman. Each is known by name and his image identified by a symbol, gesture, or posture. The time covered by this sequence of "conquerors," Jinas, is reckoned by ages, not mere centuries. Jain theology occupies a middle ground between that of Hinduism and Buddhism, sharing beliefs and practices with both. Jain temples, the earlier rock-cut ones as well as the later buildings, resemble those built during the same period and in the same locality by the other creeds.

The figure in the temple opposite is one of the Jain teachers; an ideal ascetic, stark naked as becomes one of the "air-clothed." He stands tall and perfectly straight; his eyes show he is in a deep trance. So perfect is his meditation, so deep, so true, that he is not even conscious of vines whose tendrils have twined themselves around his legs and thighs. Hooded cobras guard him, and female divinities attend him.

The Jains have one type of temple wholly their own, the "four-faced," so called because it houses not one image but four—either a quadruple image of a single Jain leader or images of four different ones standing back to back. The multiple images caused changes within the "holy of holies," transforming the dark, mysterious sanctum with its single door into open, well-lighted niches. Each of the four images had its doorway,

Jain rock-cut sanctuary. *Vitold de Golish, from* The Golden Age of Indian Art

looking out on porches which led directly to the courtyard and permitting the light to surround and irradiate the inner shrine.

Early in their history the Jains singled out "mountains of immortality." On some they placed simple shrines where they could "worship the mountains as the feet of Jina"; on others they built a single temple, imposing and sizable; and on still others they built their so-called temple cities—hundreds of shrines and temples crowded onto a lofty site, to ornament, as they say, "these holy hills with a crown of eternal Arhat *chaityas* [chapels for saints] shining with the splendor of jewels." Among their holiest and most famous mountains is Girnar *(below)*. Every precious inch of level ground has been planted with sacred monuments; several are clustered together within the protection of fortress-like parapets which were manned when invaders overran the country. It is, as it were, a city of temples. No human beings dwell there, and at nightfall, when the pilgrim throngs leave, only the gods remain in their houses high on the sacred hill.

Jain temple city, Mount Girnar

The powerful impulses generated by Buddhism unified the many different peoples to whom India extended her civilization. Indian religions triumphed over the nature gods worshiped in Ceylon, Burma, Cambodia, Thailand, and Java, those lands rimming the Indian Ocean which have been grouped together as Greater India.

With each creed went its sacred writings, myths, and images, its rituals and ceremonies, and above all, the basic plans for its temples. Buddhist missionaries brought not only holy relics and the Buddhist Path to enlightenment and emancipation, but the meaning and form of the stupa as well. Hindu priests migrated with Aryan tribes into new territories, where the towered sanctuary and the sculptured presentation of their gods and cosmic myths were re-created in magnificent structures. Borobudur and Angkor Wat (originally consecrated to Vishnu) are two of the masterpieces of Greater India.

The awakening produced by the impact on native talents of the advancing Indian civilization resulted in sacred monuments at once related and markedly individual. In part, the variations can be traced to changes within Buddhism: thus, the missionaries of the Hinayana period introduced the semiglobular stupa; while the later ones, who proclaimed the universal salvation offered by Mahayana Buddhism, introduced images of the Buddhas and Bodhisattvas. But the sacred structures were subtly but unmistakably altered to allow the peoples who created them to express their traditional ideas of divine majesty and royal splendor and beauty.

The power generated by Mahayana Buddhism radically changed Asia. So extraordinary was its impulse that it was able to impart its faith to distant China, a region already possessed of an ancient and distinctive civilization. A four-hundred-year-old religious system complete with sects—each with its own priests, monastic orders, and rituals—was transferred from India to China, and huge quantities of sacred commentaries and images were transported. In this process, the creed's center of gravity shifted and the stupa's form was radically altered: Indian themes were reworked to satisfy Far Eastern temperaments and cultures. Where the Indian had Nirvana as his goal, the Chinese often had the Western Paradise; where the Indian approached the historical Buddha, Sakyamuni, through the disciplines of austere meditation, the Chinese and Japanese often relied on a daily invocation of the gracious Amitabha Buddha, the compassionate deity of the Pure Land sect. And, architecturally, where the Indian expressed the ultimate mystery in the stupa, with a profusion of shrines clustered about, the

Chinese, on the other hand, planned their temples in simple, symmetrical geometric forms.

Geography was a hurdle to Buddhism's passage to the Far East. Some missionaries, continuing the long overseas voyage beyond the lands of Greater India, reached south China and gave that region a special quality. But more significant were the missionaries who went overland to the Han empire of north China. Almost fifteen hundred years before Christian monks started their heroic penetration of the Americas, Buddhist monks were crossing the Asian land mass, making their way over a vast terrain studded with mountain ranges, scarred by terrible deserts, and filled with feuding tribes. They traveled the full length of the Old Silk Road, a trail whose fragile unity depended on the passing of luxury goods from tribe to tribe. A pioneer on this precarious highway, the most famous of the Han ambassadors, Chang Ch'ien, took twelve years (138–126 B.C.) to make his way to the Bactrian court and return to China. Bactria had been conquered by one of the generals of Alexander the Great, and Bactria's Macedonian rulers attracted Hellenistic artists and artisans to the east. There, at Gandhara, under the succeeding Kushan dynasty, Greco-Roman sculptors adapted Western styles—the anthropomorphic tradition in Greek religious art and the idealized features and conventional drapery of the statues of the deified Roman emperors—to Buddhist uses. From Gandhara, images of the Buddha, the god in human form, were carried eastward along the Old Silk Road to China.

The intellectual barriers between Indian-born Buddhism and the Chinese were formidable. Sanskrit is a highly inflected, polysyllabic language, requiring an alphabet in its written form. The Indian mind was wont to ramble and range, and was attracted to abstract ideas, expressing them in cosmic metaphors and myths. The Chinese mind, on the other hand, cherished brevity; the metaphors congenial to its genius were pungent and familiar, and its verbal imagery was personal and concrete. The problems of making Buddhism intelligible can be glimpsed when we are told that the closest equivalent the translators had for the basic, all-embracing Sanskrit word for "morality" was the character used by the Confucians to indicate "filial submission and obedience."

Buddhism took root in China as the great Han empire was falling apart, about 220 A.D.; China was overrun by the Huns in 311. By the sixth century, early individual fervor had become an immense and influential institution. From descriptions of this vanished first flowering (there were more than four thousand monasteries, forty thousand temples and shrines, and a quarter of a million monks and nuns), we know that the forms and functions of the sacred structures were Chinese, not Indian. Scholars have noted the Chinese instinct for verticality; indeed, some have observed that the number of stories in a pagoda serves as a rough index of Buddhism's growth. In the fourth century, pagodas had three stories; in the fifth century, seven stories; and in the sixth century, nine. The imperial temple built early that century at the northern capital of Lo-yang was, with its nine-storied pagoda, the most resplendent. Sedately opulent, the pagoda was festooned with hundreds of gold bells, and its red lacquered doors—three on each of its four sides—were trimmed with rows of gold nailheads. Of the temple's several buildings, only the pagoda was not traditionally Chinese. The Buddha hall, housing an eighteen-foot gold Buddha attended by ten life-sized gold Bodhisattvas, was similar to large government office buildings; and the four gateways in the enclosing wall resembled Han watchtowers. But to the Chinese, and after them the Japanese, the pagoda was free from secular associations and uses. It symbolized the new faith. This faith became an instrument for uniting regional groups into empires subject to a single ruler. Thus, the first Sui emperor, to commemorate his victory, decreed (589) that a specially designed pagoda should be built in each province to receive its portion of newly acquired relics; and, in the same spirit, a devout Japanese emperor ordered (740) a "realm-guarding temple" for each of his provinces.

Where did it come from, this pagoda which had such meaning for its builders and which is to us the quintessence of Far Eastern architecture? This shrine, so different in form and feeling from the massive, earth-bound stupa whose function it serves, seems to have been inspired by the multistoried Kushan tower. The powerful Indo-Scythian Kushan kingdom (its capital was near the modern city of Peshawar in Pakistan) flourished during the first two centuries of the Christian era, maintaining cordial diplomatic relations with Rome; here Greco-Roman sculptors worked side by side with artists from India and Persia. The great Kushan king, Kanishka, "a second Ashoka" (c. 120–162), was Mahayana Buddhism's patron and protector, and his famous tower was the beacon that welcomed Chinese pilgrims, announcing their proximity to India, the holy land of Buddhism. It was a thirteen-storied wooden structure above which rose an iron mast bedecked with thirteen golden disks. Its simple, square, one-storied unit reminded the Chinese of their own watchtowers; its awe-inspiring height – achieved by piling one unit, roof included, on top of another in diminishing sizes – symbolized the World-Mountain, and its disked mast was the insignia of celestial royalty.

Indian rock-hewn chapels, such as the pilgrims saw at Ajanta, suggested the creation of similar architectural sculpture in China. But the original style was markedly altered by Central Asian influences as it moved eastward. Scholars exploring the abandoned Old Silk Road have discovered along its way rock-hewn chapels of large monastic communities. Undisturbed since the days when they served important religious settlements, these chapels yielded interiors lavishly decorated with holy images, carved and painted, and libraries filled with precious contemporary texts. These chapels show us the additions Central Asia made to Buddhism from the fifth to the eleventh centuries. Afghanistan contributed an intense veneration for images, a tradition carried on by Chinese and Japanese Buddhism; the Indian stupa, as an object of worship, disappears, and in its place there is an altar – that is, the place on which the images of the gods stand and around which the faithful make their devout circumambulations. From here, too, the cult of colossal images traveled to the Far East – the giant icons at Bamian are 175 and 120 feet high. These cliff-high Buddhas, sculptured, stuccoed, painted, and gilded, have moved away from the Hellenistic style: they conform to the Eastern ideal of frontality and an abstract, anti-naturalistic portrayal of the divine.

These elements of Central Asian religious practices were incorporated into the early fifth-century temple caves of north China, at Yunkang and Lungmen. (The Japanese lacked rock suitable for such architecture. They built wooden houses for the divine images, which were modeled out of clay, or cast in bronze, or carved out of wood, or formed laboriously in lacquer.) One of the wonders of the Far Eastern Buddhist world was the gigantic image carved into the cliff at Yunkang. A 45-foot Buddha, seated in the pose of deep meditation, he is the epic figure of the personal savior. To create their own mighty icon in the form and size of the Yunkang Buddha, the Japanese, about 750, in a heroic burst of religious fervor and national self-consciousness, made the huge bronze Daibutsu, or Great Buddha, at Nara. (Gold deposits found just at that time enabled them to gild the 53-foot giant, which remains the largest casting ever made in Japan.) Another Japanese treasure, the exquisite bronze Shaka triad at Horyuji—the Buddha seated between two disciples—was inspired by the same group sculptured across the rear wall of a Lungmen cave-chapel, a group considered the finest example of the archaic Buddha images in China. It was out of the plastic ingredients of Greco-Roman, Indian, Persian, and Central Asian styles—the polyglot languages of Buddhism—that the Chinese and Japanese artists formed their own art languages.

Devotion to sacred images made the Buddha hall, or golden hall, or, as the Japanese call it, the *kondo*, the focus of prayers and rituals. The hall housing the icons replaced the pagoda as the venerated heart of the temples. This shift in emphasis was sanctioned when Buddhism received the lavish patronage of the Sui and early T'ang dynasties (589–907). The magnificent temples designed by the imperial architects—the T'ang instinct was to think in "big, clear, simple terms"—had two pagodas (instead of one) placed on either side of the Buddha hall. This was a recognition of the importance of the Buddha hall, which was designed and constructed to resemble the imperial majesty of the throne hall. The glory of these vanished T'ang temples can be glimpsed in the Todaiji monastery at Nara (William Willetts refers to its present eighteenth-century reconstruction as a "shrunken and debased descendant of the mid-eighth-century original"). For Todaiji was built when Chinese doctrines and architecture still dominated the Japanese; into its construction the Japanese put their united efforts and meager resources to make it the equal of the splendid, admired Chinese model.

Buddhism, both the religion and its architecture, came to Japan from the mainland via Korea, or north China, or south China, at different times and by different routes. Not until the ninth century did Japan start her independent and brilliant formulations of Buddhist thought and architecture.

Buddhism's willingness to integrate local divinities brought it the necessary popular support. Initially its appeal had been to men of education and intellectual pursuits—in China the invention of printing was related to the rise and spread of Buddhism—and to the ruling class: in Japan the sacred monuments of the Nara period (600–794) were monuments to the newly formed national consciousness as much as they were sacred to Buddhism.

The latitude to be found within Buddhism appears to be boundless. Take, for example, the omnipresent Boddhisattvas. From local gods and "worthy ones," saintly ascetics, they became, as we have seen, agents of personal salvation, earthborn saints who had refused to take the final step out of earthly existence into Nirvana so that they might help pious suppliants ascend the upward path. In China, the Bodhisattva concept accommodated the ancient Taoist mountain-dwelling, cloud-riding nature gods. In

Japan, Buddhism merged with worship of the native Shinto pantheon to produce Ryobu Shinto, in which the so-called "eight million gods" are earthly manifestations of the indestructible Buddhist divinities. It also produced the cult of the Vairochana Buddha (known in Japan as the Dainichi Buddha) who is portrayed seated on a lotus flower of a thousand petals, each one of which represents a universe with its own Buddha: he symbolizes "galaxies of Buddha worlds."

The variety of Buddha images makes the sectarian differences instantly recognizable. The earliest ones present the historical Buddha, Sakyamuni: still a man who was born and lived, suffered, and taught, he stands on the threshold of divinity, his life and acts touched by the miraculous and superhuman. The later ones show that the transition has been made: he is no longer a person to be venerated, but the god to be worshiped.

The temples themselves, in their very designs, state their sectarian beliefs. Octagonal pagodas, for example, are dedicated to the Buddha Vairochana. As the spectrum of sectarian beliefs is vast, so is their associated architecture. At one extreme are the spectacular and florid Buddhist gods of Tibet in their wrathful aspects, at the other the severely elegant shrines built by the Japanese Zen Buddhists.

Tibetans venerate the Dalai Lama, who is thought of as the reincarnated Avalokiteshvara, greatest and best-loved Bodhisattva of the Buddha Amitabha; therefore, his former residence, the Potala, had the sacred aura of a shrine. The Lamaistic church stresses the efficacy of occult, magical formulas and places, an ardent emphasis on rituals; it has absorbed primitive Hindu beliefs in demonology and female energies as well as Asian shamanistic practices. Tibetan stupas—half Indian stupa, half Chinese pagoda—elongated, bottle-shaped monuments that look as though they had been turned on the lathe of strong mountain winds, usually mark the graves of Lamaist saints.

Like the other sects, Zen came to Japan from China. It is neither the oldest nor the most widespread of the Buddhist sects within Japan, but its doctrine is the one best known outside. A contemplative sect in which each man works out his own inner realization, Zen is meditative and deeply metaphysical and imposes far-reaching mental and physical disciplines on its followers. Its few early buildings in Japan are chapels, or small hillside retreats, whose isolation preserved them from destruction during the decades of civil war, when embattled monks razed the temples of rival sects. The uniformity of its later temples—the two gateways, Buddha hall, and lecture hall spaced along a straight north-south line, with the library and the houses for the bell, drum, and bathing arranged symmetrically with other secondary buildings on either side—is rooted in Zen's firm adherence to hallowed Chinese originals. This master plan is revealed in the manuscript copies of notes and drawings made by a Japanese pilgrim who spent four years in China (1259–1263) noting precisely and minutely monastic rules, ritual furnishings, and architectural construction. Maintaining the traditional arrangement did not confine the creative genius of Zen Buddhists. Rather, their doctrine encouraged them to charge scenes and acts with ceremony to promote mental composure and enlightenment. Their tea ceremony, specially housed and performed with ritual meticulousness, and their landscape gardening—ranging from exquisite miniatures of nature to mystical abstractions—have profound religious meanings, learned by direct experience.

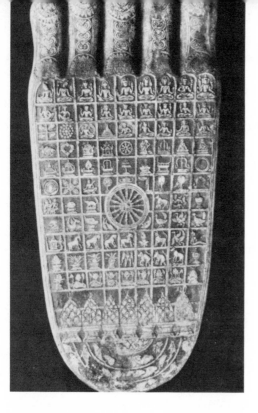

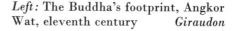

Left: The Buddha's footprint, Angkor Wat, eleventh century   *Giraudon*

We can follow the spread of Buddhism across the waters of the Indian Ocean and the vast width of Asia. The footprint at left, a symbol commonly used in Hinayana Buddhism, carries the iconographic alphabet of Mahayana Buddhism as it was used in Indochina.

Ceylon

The Emperor Ashoka sent his son Mahinda to carry the message of Buddhism to the king of Ceylon, and, except for a short period, 900–1150 A.D., when Indian invaders forced Hinduism on the country, Ceylon remained Buddhist. Anuradhapura, the capital of that flourishing island kingdom, welcomed the princely missionary; there religious establishments of phenomenal size were constructed. "Dagoba," the Sinhalese word for stupa, is a contraction of a term meaning "relic-chamber." The dagobas of Ceylon have their own characteristics, a particular rhythm of square and round units. The high semiglobular dagoba stands on three concentric circular terraces, which in turn stand on a large square terrace approached by a flight of stairs set in the middle of each side. Above the mound, square, circle, and spire, diminished in size, taper to hold the finial.

Twenty-two centuries old, stripped of architectural refinements and overgrown with grass and shrubs, the dagobas of Anuradhapura, such as the one shown on the opposite page, left, seem more like a part of the forested landscape than man-made shrines. Many thousand feet in circumference and more than 250 feet high, it suggests the care and skill and labor that went into the foundations, which support a mass equal to that of the Menkure pyramid at Giza. The pious King Duthagamini supervised the work at Anuradhapura: he ordered, an ancient chronicle recorded, "round stones to be brought by his soldiers, had them well beaten down with pounders, and to ensure greater durability he caused that layer of stones to be trampled by enormous elephants whose feet were protected by leathern shoes. He had clay spread upon the layer of stones: over them a network of iron: over that a layer of *phalika* stone, and over that he laid a course of

Anuradhapura   *Paul Popper Ltd.*   Ruanweli dagoba, Anuradhapura   *Viollet*

common stones." Then the king, in royal splendor, accompanied by a throng of female
dancers and singers, a band of musicians, and forty thousand men, ceremonially laid the
first brick of the dagoba.

The spacious square inner terrace of the Ruanweli dagoba *(above, right)* was oriented
to the cardinal points and decorated with a frieze of elephants facing outward. The
customary threetiered circular terraces show a feature peculiar to Ceylon: a diminutive
chapel placed on a ledge and reached by a short flight of steps. Such model-sized chapels housed additional holy relics; unlike the austerely plain white plaster coating of
mound and spire, these were charmingly decorated with carvings and delicate mold-
ings and brightened with color and gilt.

But the focal point of the sacred monument was placed high up at the very top of the
mound: in a special compartment the Mystic Stone was placed. We do not know whether the spire was the honorific parasol furled to look like a staff or the sacred pillar worshiped by Ceylon's aboriginal inhabitants, the Veddas. Whatever its original meaning,
it became the seal and emblem of the dagoba's sanctity.

The south Indian invaders destroyed as much as they could of the vast Buddhist
establishments at Anuradhapura. In temples built to their Hindu gods they disdained
the native preference for brick as a building material and, as was their tradition, constructed their temples out of stone. The god Shiva is shown on the following page and
close to him, as always, his white bull, the gentle, patient Nandi, carved in the lyric
style of Mahabalipuram.

Shiva: relief on rock temple, Anuradhapura   *Photos: Paul Popper Ltd.*

The Sinhalese expelled the Indians at the start of the twelfth century, and their king built dagobas at Polonnaruva, his new capital *(below)* to celebrate the return to Buddhism. Their style is at once a sad and clumsy restatement of the earlier architectural mastery and the tentative start of a new idiom. Essentially the dagoba's design remains, but its altered proportions give it a new and different emphasis: the concentric terraces gain in importance; the mound, reduced almost to a token, no longer overwhelms the worshiper but rather invites him to contemplation. The colonnades of freestanding pillars vociferously restate an ancient sacred theme; the stele-shaped relief panels, with the conventionalized carvings of divine door-guardians with which the balustrades are finished, are reminiscent of Indian temples.

Small stupa atop the rock, Konzi

Burma

Remains of early stupas, as at Konzi *(above)*, indicate that the Burmese genius forged its own architectural language out of those which flowed into that vast delta region from India and China. The Burmese master masons were glad to use both the convex curve of the Indian stupa and tower and the inward sweep, the concave line, of the Chinese pagoda. The *hti*, the Burmese version of the honorific umbrella that served as the finial, has its distinctive profile etched against the sky.

Scholars have distinguished an "early phase" in Burmese sacred monuments, from the second century A.D. to the beginning of the ninth. The "classical," from the ninth through the thirteenth centuries, is wholly contained in the temples at Pagan, built when that city, the product of religious zeal and nationalist fervor, was the capital of a united people. Over four hundred years, without pause or a slackening of energy, more than ten thousand sacred monuments dedicated to Hinayana Buddhism, many of considerable size, were built there. Much of this vast, lush garden of temples and shrines has been marvelously preserved.

Conquest by the Chinese ushered in the "pagoda period." Thereafter, as at Prome *(see page 67)*, Burmese temples were made mostly of wood; they have the intimate quality of a joyous folk art.

Thuparama temple, Polonnaruva

The Thatbyinyu temple at Pagan *(opposite)*, is basically a cruciform design, occupying a huge area and rising over 150 feet from the ground to its topmost *hti,* above the main spire. The graduated terraces, the tapering volume of the ascending mass, its complex, projecting porticos show a disciplined planning. This architectural sobriety can be overlooked by visitors. The hot sun throws a confusing pattern of shadow-black lines on its glittering whiteness, and everywhere the straight line is embellished with curves, spirals, and foliations, and the eye is distracted by lavish color.

Great Pagoda at Prome

Opposite: Thatbyinyu temple, Pagan. *Mella*

However far removed the Shwe Dagon at Rangoon *(left)* is from the earth-hugging mound of the classical stupa at Sanchi, it is related in spirit. Set upon a stepped terrace more than 400 feet in diameter, the 370-foot spire, slim and tapering, rises in an undulating line; the simple expedient of horizontal grooves enables it to combine pleasingly the Indian curve with that of China. This most venerated stupa-pagoda was built in the mid-sixteenth century on a terrace whose holiness was very old; within its relic-chamber it holds a hallowed treasure—eight sacred hairs of the Buddha.

Around it, narrowing the ambulatory, is a cluster of structures that repeat in miniature the central spire; the base of the spire, as high as arms can reach, sprouts a jungle of paper *htis* and *tagunlones*, as shown below, and wears a jumble of glass, wood and metal, gilt and paint.

Shwe Dagon, Rangoon *Mella* *Paul Popper Ltd.*

Htis, parasols, and *tagunlones*, snakelike streamers, placed as votive offerings at Shwe Dagon

Jungle temple, Sawankhalok   *Hürlimann*

Thailand

Soon after the Thais moved southward into the vast country to which they gave their
name, they built the now jungle-ruined temple shown above, at Sawankhalok. Some
scholars see in such temples a provincial version of the great Khmer architecture of
Cambodia; others find that its style echoes monuments at Polonnaruva, then newly built
in Ceylon.

We can still see traces of the colonnade of pillars which formed an avenue leading to
the beautifully carved colossal Buddha. Originally a thick wall, pierced here and there
by long thin apertures, acted as a screen through which the worshiper viewed the image.
And behind the seated figure, just topping it, was an attenuated stupa, here called a
pra-prang.

69

One of the colossal Buddhas, 175 feet high, at Bamian, third century

Afghanistan

The oasis of Bamian was occupied by a Buddhist sect whose creed stressed the divine nature of the Buddha. The more-than-mortal became here the larger-than-life-size statue – as in Rome, where Nero had a 120-foot statue of himself placed at the entrance to his palatial Golden House.

The folds of the Buddha's gigantic garment were formed on cords hung from pegs socketed in the stone and encased in stucco. The niche behind the statue was painted with the myriad manifestations of the Buddha.

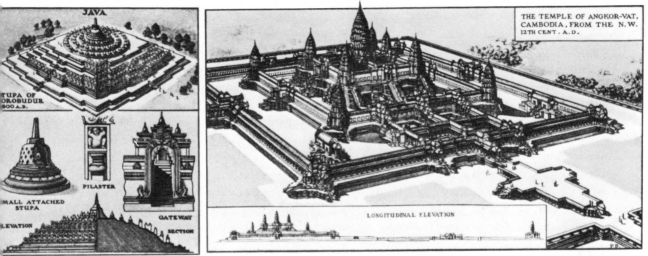

Percy Brown

Java and Cambodia

In the magnitude of their architectural conception and execution and the beauty and extent of their sculptured surfaces, Borobudur and Angkor Wat take their places among the very finest of the great houses raised and decorated by man for his gods to dwell in. At once vast and intricate, they defeat the camera, which at best can only indicate their grandeur or catch a tiny fraction of the stupendous visions realized in stone.

Java's Borobudur, or "Many Buddhas," is the island's only impressive structure. From a gentle knoll, the great stupa looks over a pleasant countryside of wooded hills and tended rice fields to a ring of mountains beyond, where pillars of smoke lazily point out still-active volcanoes. An iridescent golden light falls over fields and sanctuary as the tropical sunshine passes through the prism-like atmosphere of volcanic vapor.

Mountains and monument are formed of the same material. Boulders spewed out in an eruption were cut into blocks, painstakingly smoothed by hand; block was fitted to block without mortar, and finally the pitted surface was hidden under a plaster wash. Once, it is thought, color was applied to the sculptured figures.

Borobudur's plan *(see above, left)* is essentially simple. Three great square terraces—the lowest measures 500 feet on each side—rising like a stepped pyramid are connected by stairs which mount steeply through carved doorways. Each terrace becomes an open corridor, on both sides of which are wonderfully carved friezes—thirteen hundred in all—offering the worshiper spiritual nourishment. Above the square terraces are three circular ones, also diminishing in size as they ascend: on them, at regular intervals, seventy-two small stupas are placed. And finally, the quiet climax of devotion and reassurance, raised over a hundred feet above the ground on this pedestal of square and round terraces, is the large, traditionally plain stupa.

71

It is a good hundred years since Henri Mouhot, a French naturalist exploring the unknown flora and fauna of the dense Cambodian jungle, stumbled upon the extraordinary ruins of Angkor Wat, of whose very existence nothing had been known. Since then archaeologists and scholars have labored to restore the forgotten Khmers to history. We know that two groups of invaders—Indo-Aryans (who brought their primitive Hinduism and its sacred language, Sanskrit) and Mongolians (the spoken language belongs to the Chinese-Tibetan family)—mixed with the aboriginal population and by the beginning of the sixth century A. D. were on their way to imperial stature. The Khmer empire was at its dazzling height during the twelfth century, when Angkor Wat, whose meaning is "city temple" or, we would say, "grand cathedral," was built. A Chinese resident of the walled capital, Angkor Thom, left a record of Khmer society, its refinement and elegance, its cultural aspirations, and its artistic and intellectual ability. The empire's finale was swift, terrible, and complete: by 1431 the Khmers had been conquered by the Thais. The people drifted away from their cities and gradually lost even the memory of their past greatness. Then the unopposed vegetal force of the jungle threw a screen around the abandoned temples and palaces and remorselessly leveled them.

Angkor Wat is the architectural glory of a people whom Percy Brown has hailed as "one of the greatest building races in the world." The temple's sacred space *(see page 71, right)*, covering a square three-fifths of a mile long on each side, was enclosed by a moat 650 feet wide whose over-all length was two and a half miles. The soil excavated from this formed the mound on which the square foundation platform was laid. The temple was approached by a causeway, 36 feet wide and 1500 feet long, raised above the surrounding country, paved, and with elaborately carved balustrades; it led to the single bridge crossing the moat and terminated within the temple space on a large, cross-shaped terrace set above the foundation platform. This opened directly on the intricate temple portico. Through its design of courtyards and pillared halls the colossal structure accommodated human proportions. Steep flights of steps ascended from towered terrace to towered terrace, each terrace a vast gallery lined with sculptured friezes. From the third terrace the main tower, built above the "holy of holies," soared aloft, its pinnacle a golden lotus more than 200 feet above the ground.

The jungle mauled Angkor Wat but did not obliterate its majestic architectural order and balance—a series of rectangles concentrically arranged to form a series of graduated terraces with towers at the angles to give vertical emphasis and prepare the worshiper's eye for the largest and highest tower over the central sanctuary. What distinguishes the firm simplicity of its design is not the magnitude of the imagination, not the prodigious labor required, not even Angkor Wat's immensity, but the sense of rhythm, now lively, now languorous, which the Khmer genius gave to the temple.

The temple's bas-reliefs depict the rich Hindu mythology, but in terms of the thirteenth-century aristocratic Khmer life almost as it was observed by the Chinese visitor. The eighteen thousand sculptured scenes lining the corridors are arranged in a continuous frieze 2000 feet long and 6 feet high. Whereas the plastic art carved on the walls of Borobudur is round, robust, and bold, that of Angkor Wat is as smooth as a tapestry. Here the traditional Indian Hindu themes are placed in a Cambodian setting.

The Potala, Lhasa   *Hürlimann*

Tibet

The Potala at Lhasa *(above)*, was the principal residence of the Dalai Lama, who Tibetans believe is a living Bodhisattva. Lamaism came to Tibet, so tradition has it, when
in the seventh century the king of Lhasa took one wife from Nepal and one from China—
a legend that explains the Buddhist influences from India and the Chinese-inspired theo-
cratic nature of the state.

A European visitor to Tibet has suggested that the inward tilt of such impressive
buildings gives them their quality of belonging to the rocky outcropping on which
they are always perched.

The Kum Bum chapel *(overleaf)* is one of Tibet's most venerated sanctuaries. Surrounded by a great number of chapels and temples and monastic installations, this
stupa—the Tibetan word is *chorten*—stands above a unique temple. The gradually widening tiers under the stupa hold chapels, seventy-three in all; each is decorated in the
highly stylized Tibetan manner. In its entirety, through the form of its stupa and the
sacred themes of its chapel paintings, the Kum Bum presents the Tibetan image of the
universe.

73

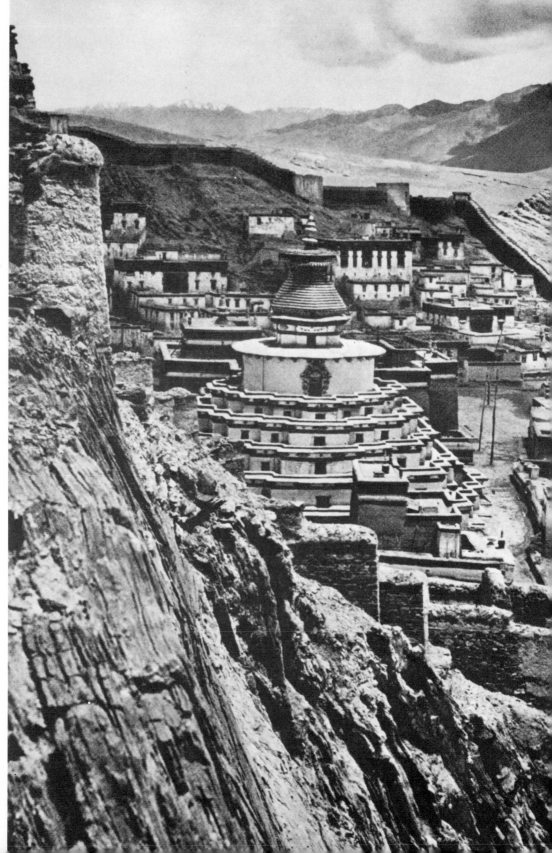

Gyangtse monastery, Tibet, with the Kum Bum *chorten.*
Hürlimann

China

The style of Buddhist places of worship was changed by Buddhism's journey across Central Asia. This can be seen below in the caves of Chienfotung *(top, left and right)*, Yunkang *(bottom, left)*, and Lungmen *(bottom, right)*, in western China.

The palette used in painting the caves had gray, a dark red, maroon, and purple, set off by touches of cream and light blue. Needham, who noted the color scheme, also remarks that some of the monks and lay worshipers there have brown and red hair and blue or green eyes, and that their features are noticeably Occidental.

The seated figure at lower left, deep in meditation, is thought to be the Buddha Amitabha, who presides over the Western Paradise, an utterly desirable region of palaces and gardens, jewel-bearing trees, flowers, fruits, and birds.

Paul Popper Ltd.   *Hürlimann*

British Museum   *Hoppenot*

The Great Pagoda,
Chengsden

Hürlimann

Temple of Heaven, Peking

The unadorned Temple of Heaven, at Peking *(above)*, has been called the most sacred of all Chinese religious buildings. Here the emperor, the Son of Heaven, to prove his filial virtue to the empire, sacrificed a bullock at the winter solstice—the sacrifice due his imperial ancestors—and worshiped Heaven, the supreme Parent.

Temple of Five Pagodas, near Peking

Hoppenot

Temple of Polola at Chengteh (Jehol)

Taoist shrine at Tai Shan

Hürlim

Tai Shan *(right)*, a mountain shrine, gatehouse, enclosure, and Buddha hall, illustrates Buddhism's ability to absorb and pre-empt earlier, native Taoist cults. The mountain itself was one of the most sacred in China, for here, the Taoists believed, the Immortals gathered. At its summit men could hope for supernatural favors: the phoenixes (one of the Objects of Good Omen) would assemble; the pure would see the divine men, perhaps be preserved forever, their longevity be of ten thousand years.

Taoism itself, on the one hand, retained the ancient Chinese belief in fertility and nature gods and in magical and shamanistic rituals and beliefs; this was the Taoism known and practiced by the great body of the Chinese people. On the other hand, as Needham has stressed, the Taoists included a small

Tomb of Confucius in the family shrine, Kufu
Hürlimann

group of highly intelligent men who, as philosophers, opposed the Confucian ideal of a perfect,
ordered society by stressing the need to discover
the "Order of Nature." The fusion of two such dis-
parate attitudes was possible because in its forma-
tive stage science is indistinguishable from magic:
as the science of chemistry in the West evolved out
of the labors of the alchemists, so in China, the
compass was first used in geomancy, a form of
divination.

The socially-minded Confucius (551–479 B.C.) was
an inspired teacher; though he was an agnostic and
rationalist, the cult of the nature gods intruded on
his teachings after his death and became an integral part of Confucianism. Thus, it was said, a
unicorn (also, with the phoenix, the tortoise, and
the dragon, one of the Objects of Good Omen)
appeared at the time the sage was born. Ancestor-
worship was added, too: the first Han emperor,
about 200 B.C., honored the sage by performing the
sacrifice of an ox, a sheep, and a pig at the family
shrine. Two hundred and fifty years later, another
emperor ordered annual sacrifices to Confucius
offered in every school throughout the land. Thus,
this model of scholars became the scholars' "patron
saint" and attained the semidivine stature needed
for a hero-cult. Confucian ceremonies, lasting from
midnight to dawn, were conducted by local officials
and scholars, since the notion of a priesthood was
utterly alien to men nourished on the revered words
of the Teacher of Ten Thousand Generations.

Temple of Paijuntien
Hoppenot

Japan

The Todaiji shrine at Nara is the center for the Ritsu sect, whose founding under imperial encouragement and favor gave it the status of an official religion. One of Japan's
major Buddhist monuments, it is also revered as the temple where the monk Gangin
spent the last years of his life. The shrine commemorates this fact just as the treasures it
contains still speak of the first high moment in Japanese art; it is part of the meaning
of Nara itself. The introduction of Buddhism into Japan was second in importance only
to that of writing, and the changes which Buddhism brought affected the very fabric of
Japanese culture, enriching it in every way.

The Ritsu stood apart from other Buddhist sects. They stressed submission to the
monastic rule—that is the meaning of the word *ritsu*—and the observance of precepts and
rituals transmitted by strict and proper spiritual succession. A monk or nun had to be
ordained by properly qualified priests, and the ordination ceremony had to be performed on a *kaidan*, a special platform whose design and purpose had been formed in
India. Therefore, before the Ritsu sect could be established in Japan, it needed a priest
qualified to inaugurate the spiritual succession and to supervise and sanctify the *kaidan*.

To this end, two monks sailed to China in 733 to beg the famed and holy monk Gangin
to come to Japan. The moving story of how Gangin kept his promise to come—an effort
covering twenty years and succeeding after five attempts thwarted by everything from
pirates to shipwreck—testifies to the urgency of the mission and the fortitude and perse-
verance of the Buddhist missionaries. He reached Japan in 753, old, blind, accompanied
by disciples and a cargo of holy writings and images. An imperial decree prescribed the
place, ritual, and institutional procedure of the ordination ceremony. At Nara, the
capital city, the *kaidan* was erected in the great hall of the Todaiji Monastery, a hall
284 feet long, 166 feet wide, and 152 feet high—the Hall of the Great Buddha *(opposite)*,
the mighty symbol of a nation united under the imperial will and belief in the Buddha.

How stately and solemn that first ordination ceremony must have been—the blind
holy man receiving the long procession of novices led by the dowager-empress and, behind them, underscoring the sect's prescribed tenets, a number of monks and nuns whose
previous admission to the religious life had been ruled irregular.

81

The "Golden Pavilion" Kinkakuji, at Kyoto, is an organic part of the landscape in which the building is placed. And the landscape itself in its arrangement of trees and shrubs, rocks, and water was laid out to follow the considered artistry and abstruse symbolism of the Ming manner. The Pavilion, rebuilt in 1955, is exquisitely and daringly designed to suggest winged lightness. It was built originally in the fourteenth century, as the country villa of a nobleman. Its first floor, harmonious and delicate, was where the owner and his elegant friends paid homage to the muses of poetry and music; the upper story, its room designed in the Zen style, bare of ornament, was covered with pure gold leaf. This was the shrine where the sacred image was housed.

In China, from which the Japanese learned the Indian concept of seeking the Buddha through meditation, the Zen principles had been summed up:

A special transmission outside the scriptures,
No dependence upon the written word,
Direct pointing at the soul of man,
Seeing one's nature and attaining Buddhahood.

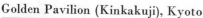

Golden Pavilion (Kinkakuji), Kyoto

Ryoanji Garden, Kyoto   *Photos: Hürlimann*

The Ryoanji Contemplation Garden at Kyoto *(above)* has the shape and size of a tennis court; its only plants are mosses cushioning the stones planted there. It is indifferent to the changing seasons: timeless. Fifteen rocks of varying forms arranged in five clusters, it might be described in Blake's lines, "a World in a Grain of Sand,/And a Heaven in a Wild Flower." Built about 1500, it is a garden for mystics to contemplate, to find therein, each for himself, his place in the spiritual universe.

We are not certain when ancestor worship reached Japan from China. Its coming established the Sun Goddess as the celestial ancestress of the imperial line, the "heavenly-sun-succession." Her shrine is the imperial family shrine and it houses the Sacred Mirror, which is venerated because the Sun Goddess gave it to her grandson as a divine token that she had sent him to rule. In the eighth century, Shintoism accepted Buddhism when the Sun Goddess herself, it is told, appeared to the emperor in a dream to announce that the Sun and the Buddha were the same and to give her divine approval to the placing of the Great Buddha in the capital: there was no friction when Buddhist priests served Shinto shrines.

In the shrine at Miyajima *(overleaf)*, corridors and galleries lead out over the sea so that at high tide the temple seems to float upon the water. *Miya* is the Japanese word

Shinto temple at Miyajima   *Ursula Bagel*

for shrine; compounded from *ya*, "House," and the honorific prefix *mi*, it suggests that the native shrine had the same form as the early dwelling house. At Ise the Great Shrines, hallowed examples of primitive thatched wood huts such as the one shown opposite, are pulled down every twenty years and faithfully rebuilt in their original style. Thus they are religious edifices at once very ancient and very recent.

The Great Shrines are great in holiness, not size. They are only large enough for an altar and priests to tend it. The worshiper stands outside, makes his obeisance–bowing deeply or clapping his hands–says a simple formulaic prayer, and presents his offerings of food, drink, and *gohei*–strips of paper attached to a wand. These, symbolic offerings replacing the cloth strips originally represented, by a kind of sacred contagion became themselves representations of the divinities, sacred objects holding spirits; after the priests have distributed them, they are placed on household altars and worshiped.

More impressive than the simple acts of worship are the purification rituals, which are of great antiquity and still obligatory before prayers can be said and offerings made. Defilement, whether accidental, natural, or deliberate, makes the individual "guilty" or "sinful," and must be removed. Exorcism is a cleansing by magical rituals performed by a priestly exorcist. Purification by ablutions or token sprinklings of water and salt–every shrine has a font in its courtyard where the worshipers wash their hands and rinse their mouths–removes pollution by accidental contact with unclean things. And, lastly, there is purification by abstention, achieved by avoiding anything that might defile.

As purity is at the heart of Shinto rites, so at the heart of all Shinto beliefs is the cult of fertility, represented at Ise by the Shrine of the Rich-Food Goddess. The popular creed expressed in a "God of the Rice," a phallic stone placed at the edge of a field, differs from the official cult, which in historical times has taken on other colorations. The blessings asked from the Shinto deities–and the "eight million gods" include every perceptible aspect of nature from the sun to mud–are those proper to farmers and fishermen. The prayers at the Harvest Festival list "crops in ears long and in ears abundant, things growing in the great moor-plain, sweet herbs and bitter herbs, things that dwell in the blue sea-plain, the broad of fin and the narrow of fin, seaweed from the offing, seaweed from the shore." Food is the theme of other important festivals: the Divine Tasting, the Tasting Together, and, especially, the solemn Great Food Offering, an elaborate thanksgiving ceremony performed by each new emperor–the ritual which gives his rule sacramental sanction.

84   *Opposite:* Great Shrine, Ise. *Y. Watanabe*

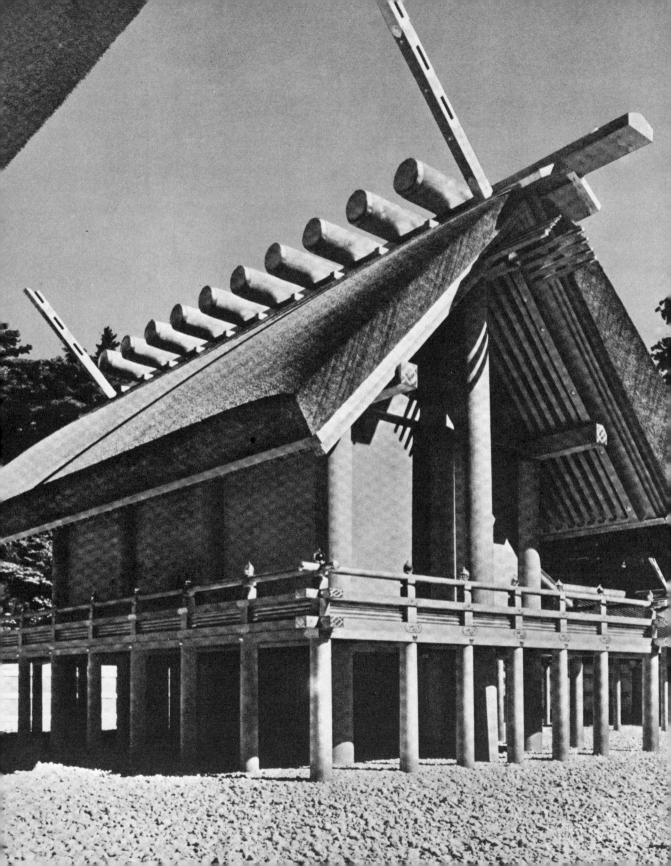

V

On Mount Olympus, beyond the sight of mortals, were the abodes of Homer's mighty gods and goddesses. In the *Odyssey* the poet identified this summit with heaven. Yet "Olympus," we now know, was a pre-Greek word for any high mountain, and therefore, in historical times, there were almost two dozen peaks of that name. In recent years scholarship has cut through the darkness of pre-Homeric Greece: the deities of Mount Olympus, who once seemed to mark the beginning of Greek religious history, are now considered to have taken shape only halfway through it.

Here and there light shines on the gods of earlier centuries, connecting them with the Olympian dwellers: divinities engraved on Mycenaean seals and Cretan shrines lead back and back to the pantheons variously domiciled in the cities of the ancient Near East, to divine kings and a perpetual priesthood, to fertility goddesses, to rites of a Sacred Marriage, to the cultic worship of the phallus and navel-stone. Resemblances are discernible as well as significant changes: the continuities perceived in looking through time are eerie and extraordinary. A kinship exists between episodes in the Sumerian epic of the hero Gilgamesh—written in the third millennium B.C.—and the experiences of Odysseus; between the Olympian Hermes, the Divine Herald, the Guide to the Dead, and the herm, the name of the phallic stone set up over a tomb; among Athena, the virgin goddess of Athens, the Athena worshiped at Mycenae and Crete, and, finally, the gross-bodied, myriad-breasted Artemis, the fertility goddess of Ephesus. Holy places have a direct continuity: recent excavations have found that the sites most sacred to classical Greece—the temple at Eleusis and Apollo's temple at Delphi—were built over Mycenaean ruins.

The differences between Homer's gods and those of antiquity are thoroughgoing and consistent. Not only did the Homeric religion ignore the divinity of kings; it also expressed the sensibilities of the Heroic Age and its warlike aristocracy by disapproving of peasant indecencies, of superstitions, cruelty, and obscenity. At worst, Homer's deities had foibles, magnified but still very human; they were amorous, willful, vainglorious, and touchy. A multitude of tribal and local divinities were absorbed into the Olympic pantheon; male gods were absorbed into the greater, more clearly defined figures of Zeus, Apollo, or Poseidon and, regardless of their places of origin, domiciled on Mount Olympus. Such celestial uprooting and engrafting reflect the momentous social change

Opposite: Snake Goddess, faïence statuette
from Knossos, MM III. *R. G. Hoegler*

Temple of Apollo, Delphi   *Mella*

brought about when the invaders violated existing tribal patterns and dispersed peoples formerly united to their gods and their kin. The heavens bear witness—like Zeus, the new masters bedded down with native women. Gradually, out of upheaval, mixing, and merging, came the political community. The polis, the Greek city-state, eventually replaced tribal cohesion. And as the tribe had had divine sanction and identity, so the polis had sacred and personal significance for the inhabitants who lived clustered within its hallowed walls.

The *Iliad* and the *Odyssey* were never sacred books. Nevertheless, to the ordinary Greek citizen they had an authority similar to the Bible's influence on the English imagination: they provided a common, familiar source from which their social thinkers could draw ideas and ideals and their writers imagery and rhetoric. Scattered throughout the epics are incidents which gave the Greeks a measure of the distance that separated their enlightened worship from the bestialities of primitive rites. Homer created a religious climate, invigorating and sunlit, which invited the intellect to range, to inquire, grope, and grow—a climate unique for its lack of orthodoxy. The religion had no creed, dogmas, or any god-given commandments. Explaining how this came about—this so properly called "Greek miracle"—Jane Harrison, a student of Greek religion, wrote that it "was developed not by priests nor by prophets nor by saints . . . it was developed by poets and artists and philosophers." And again, that the Homeric religion affirmed that except for immortality, an attribute of the gods alone, "the gods were like men and men able to be godlike." In this belief Greek sculptors carved the Olympian deities not as a monstrous sphinx, scaly serpent, or Minotaur, but as divine excellence in human form.

Such statues of the gods—Zeus, Apollo, and Athena; Poseidon, Hera, and Hermes—carved, painted, and gilded, were sheltered in temples dedicated to their worship. Greek temples still speak sublimely to us, though mutilated and abandoned. Some of the serene beauty of a temple lies in its location, chosen, it might be thought, so that it can dominate the scene while yet remaining a part of it. But temple and site have more than an aesthetic relationship: they are joined together by the coexistence of pre-Greek and Greek holiness, for invisible but present are the ancient gods and goddesses who reside under the monuments sacred to the invader's deities. The site itself was the hallowed part: it was thought to have been chosen as an abode by a supernatural being that, with rare exception, was pre-Greek. On this divinely chosen spot the temple was superimposed. If the temple was destroyed, nothing had suffered desecration; a new edifice served equally well to shelter the site.

But if the Greeks permitted the old gods to remain in their earthly abodes, the temples they built to their deities have no connection with pre-Greek architecture. Deliberately, it must seem, they did not avail themselves of the traditional high-vaulted masonry of the Mycenaean Greek *tholos*, a notable architectural achievement derived from the Near East. The marble masterpieces we admire evolved out of the simple, timbered rectangular house form whose design and construction belonged to the forested Europe the invaders had inhabited before they moved into Greece. Whether in the earliest shrines still made out of tree trunks split and covered with wattle, or in limestone temples stuccoed over and painted, or in the colonnaded Parthenon, the sculptured Erechtheum, and other marble sanctuaries; whether in Athens, holy Delphi, or any of the Greek overseas, away-from-home cities, the Greeks consistently carried on, elaborated, and beautified a constructional system of posts and beams derived from European timber prototypes.

In temples bathed in bright sunlight, the statues of the Homeric gods were sheltered. But here and there, in ever-mounting boldness, the old divinities emerged from the earth to walk about. Their cults were popular, welcoming women as well as men, slave as well as free man to the ranks of initiates. So irresistible was the appeal of the Eleusinian and Orphic Mysteries, as these new religions were called, that they became official by classical times. Annually the people of Athens marched in solemn procession to nearby Eleusis to honor Demeter, the venerable goddess of vegetation. Annually the Orphic Mysteries, centered on Dionysus, were celebrated at Delphi.

Dionysus at Delphi: his presence there is most strange, as his enshrining is characteristically Greek. This alien god of the vine, this god of excess whose cultic orgies inflamed his followers to frenzied, delirious ecstasy, the Greek genius could not tolerate. At some distant time, in some unknown place, Dionysus had a summit meeting with Apollo, the Olympian god whose motto "Nothing in excess" was graven on his Delphi shrine, to emerge metamorphosed into the god of regeneration and rebirth. Dionysus is said to have brought what the Olympian religion denied man—the promise of immortality. Demeter and Dionysus: with them the sacrament of partaking of bread and wine came into the Greco-Roman world.

The worship of Dionysus created a wholly new kind of temple: the theater; and the Dionysia, the ceremonies of his worship, grew into the great dramatic festival of Athens. The theater provided a place where an audience could see and hear the sorrowful story of the god's suffering, death, and resurrection: and the audience, aroused to pity and awe by the drama they beheld, were, as one, lifted to a mystical ecstasy. "The Delphic way and the way of Dionysus reached their perfect union in the fifth-century theater," according to Jane Harrison. "There the great mystery, human life, was presented through the power of great art. Poet and actors and audience were conscious of a higher presence. They were gathered there in an act of worship, all sharing in the same experience."

Rome's marble temples built during the Principate of Augustus, 27 B.C. to 14 A.D., show the imperial Roman temper. Clustered around the Forum, they are the religious aspect of Rome's political life—purposeful, proud of the peace Rome had created and maintained, and tolerant of her empire's many divinities, whatever their origin and import. Augustus, the title assumed by the first emperor, signifies "auspicious" as well as "eminent" and "revered"; his name was Octavian—E. M. Forster brands him as "one of the most odious of the world's successful men." During his lifetime his birthday was celebrated with solemn thanksgiving (giving his name to our month of August) and his cult, Rome and Augustus, formally instituted. His person and high office were deemed sacrosanct and the imperial cult with its official public worship of the emperor became the religious pledge of allegiance.

Augustus could boast that he had transformed a Rome of brick and masonry into a Rome of marble. His grandiose civic building program restored more than eighty temples in addition to the large number of new ones. By the Augustan Age, the Romans had infused the amalgam of architectural styles borrowed from the Greeks and Etruscans with their own innovations in structure; henceforth, they could build monuments suitable to their imperial image. (Where the Etruscans originated is still a matter of conjecture; nor have we deciphered their written language. We do know that they dominated the Italian peninsula before the Italic tribes created Rome, and from archaeological finds we have learned much about this rich, energetic, city-dwelling people and can infer the nature of their religious practices and study their art and architecture.)

Of all that Augustus built, the merest fraction remains. Archaeology has had to fill the lacunae in the structural development of Roman temples before the introduction of marble. From the Greeks the Romans borrowed the post and beam construction and the

Temple of Athena, Aegina   *Viollet*

Almost nineteen hundred years ago Plutarch marveled that such
structures as the temple of Athena at Aegina *(above)*, built in a short
time, were yet built for the ages, and as soon as they were finished had
the venerable air of antiquity. Their beauty, animated by the spirit of
perpetual youth and unfading elegance, still moves us.

stately rows of columns; their standardized system of arch, vault, and dome they inherited from the Etruscans. For a long time the Roman republic was dependent on skilled Greek workmen imported from Sicily; the oldest datable public building, a late fourth-century-B.C. temple dedicated to an unknown divinity, has identifiable masons' marks cut in the tufa blocks. In this same site archaeologists found fragments of thin plaques of fired clay, terra-cotta revetments used as ornamental protection to cover exposed wooden beams, a technique learned from the Etruscans and continued in Roman building practices until marble was introduced. Between this earlier shrine of masonry blocks set without mortar and the marble grandeur of imperial structures, the Romans had discovered and perfected the use of concrete.

Concrete was a momentous discovery. In exploiting its potentials, the Romans revolutionized architectural forms. Pozzuolana is the name of a volcanic sand that has the peculiar property of forming an exceedingly hard, cohesive mortar when mixed with lime. Pozzuolana concrete was a manufactured material: it was abundant and cheap, of great strength and marvelously tough. Poured and molded to any shape, it extended the possibilities of arch, vault, and dome. It enabled Roman architects to create interior space of great size and freed them from the tyranny of the one-storied Greek temples with their dark, constricted, boxlike interiors. The Greeks had cherished Pentelic marble. Where the temples were left unpainted the marble had a dazzling whiteness, while the nature of the substance yielded exquisitely fine joints and a satin-smooth finish. Concrete gave all this to the Romans and more—they could coat it with a fine marble stucco, brightening and highlighting wherever they pleased; they could pattern the surfaces of walls, vaults, and domes with brick, stone, or slabs of porphyry and richly grained marbles. Imperial Rome sheathed her temples and other public buildings in a rainbow of precious sparkling stones.

Recent archaeological investigations have discovered the first use of concrete in a major structure: the impressive Sanctuary of Fortune, built about 80 B.C. Here religion was architecturally dramatized: seven terrace levels mounted majestically to support the cult statue, which, placed at the apex, rose above the altar on which sacrifices were offered in full view of the worshiping throng. Knowledge of its now vanished glory permits us to appreciate the delight, the daring and mastery, of the Roman architects who could realize the ambitious design of the Emperor Hadrian's domed Pantheon, completed about 128 A.D. To lighten the enormous weight of its cupola (142 feet, 6 inches in both height and internal diameter) they not only coffered the ceiling—the traditional method—but also used pumice, a feather-light mineral, in making the concrete. The versatility of this manufactured building material made it especially suited to Rome's imperial construction needs: pozzuolana could be shipped to every part of the empire, where it gave the public buildings, temples included, a proper uniformity.

As Rome utilized in her sacred monuments architectural elements which had originated with the Greeks and Etruscans, so she borrowed from them ideas and institutions congenial to her religious needs. Homer inspired Vergil to compose a religious and national epic for the Romans—but the *Aeneid* did not promote ethical or intellectual values; its poetry had mundane objectives such as establishing dynastic sanctity for the emperor by furnishing Augustus with a legendary hero-ancestor, Aeneas. From Greece, Rome also adopted veneration for the polis, a celestial pantheon for her heterogeneous deities, the Hellenized Mysteries, and, when she wanted to adorn her finest temples, Greek statuary. From the Etruscans came her principal deities Tinia, Uni, and Menerva (Jupiter, Juno, and Minerva), a priest-king, and a belief in omens—foretelling the future from the reading of animal livers and the flight of birds. Notwithstanding this incorporation of alien traits, the Roman state religion took its form and content from the primitive family beliefs which saw a spirit, *numen*, in every object and in each minute act performed in working and living. The spirits, invisible, even formless, were named nevertheless, and with each use of the name went the proper prayer to be said, offering to be made, invocation to be pronounced. The tissue of religious life was contained in a multitude of precise, unchanging formulas.

By extension and aggrandizement the family cult and domestic rituals became the pattern for state cult and public ceremonies. Thus the family's reliance on omens became a public taking of the auspices to discover whether an action contemplated by the state was consonant with the gods' will. Similarly, out of the spirit of the family hearth came the holy goddess Vesta, whose fire burned on the state hearth housed in a temple tended by Vestal Virgins. As the head of the family supervised his household's religious observances, the priest-king did so for the state. When early in Roman history the king was expelled (an event remembered in the story of the rape of Lucrece), his sacerdotal office, "king of the sacred things," remained, its duties to be henceforth administered by "colleges." These were made up of ordinary citizens of the Republic, not priests. Members of the highest college, the *pontifices*, were selected for their probity to serve as custodians of the state's sacred customs and lore and their ability to administer the sacred laws governing rules of social conduct. Under their jurisdiction came the Vestal Virgins, the Augurs, who took the auspices, and the keepers of the Calendar, who assured the correct observance of games and of holidays dedicated to gods.

Against the promises and ritual pageants of the Oriental cults, the old Roman religion could not prevail. During the second century A.D. the gods and goddesses of Egypt and Syria and Persia—Cybele, the Great Mother of Asia Minor; Mithras, the invincible Persian sun god; Serapis of Alexandria; Isis and Osiris from Egypt—invaded metropolitan Rome itself. Priests marvelously attired presided over strange and disturbing rites, each sect preaching its belief in a single god, though none claimed his was the only god (henotheism, halfway between polytheism and monotheism). All the cults taught doctrines based on divine revelation, all demanded of their followers initiation and periods of asceticism, all promised victory over sin and death. And all celebrated their ceremonies under the gaze of the Roman gods. For to all these cults, so attractive in their vitality and reassurances, it seemed imperative that Rome, under whose power the continuance of the Greco-Roman civilization was assured, should not give up her traditional religion and ancient gods. For Rome had imposed on these aliens her belief that the city had attained imperial greatness under the will of its gods; when in Rome they thought as the Romans thought. Only two cults took exception: save Jews and Christians, all believed the power of Rome was eternal, and in this faith they felt safe.

Overleaf: East end of the Parthenon, 449–438 B.C. *Hürlimann*

Temple of Athena Nike, Athens   *Alinari*

Greece

Scarred by time and wars, its paint washed away, its friezes stripped off, and its tower-ing statue of Athena, sheathed in ivory and gold, gone—the beauty of the Parthenon still astonishes *(preceding pages)*. From the treatise written by one of its architects, we know that the structure itself was unique: subtle optical refinements created its vibrant sim-plicity. As a temple, too, it differed from all others. Thus a scholar, now reading Phidias' sculpture, perceives it to be the twin brother of tragedy: like Aeschylus, the images chant, "He prays to deaf heaven, none hears his cry"; and, like Sophocles, they state, "Numberless are the world's wonders, but none more wonderful than man."

A hundred years ago the temple of Athena Nike *(above)*, so small, so perfect, was reas-sembled—its stones having been used by the Turks to build defense bastions. Like the rest of the buildings on the Acropolis, it was commissioned by Pericles to commemorate the city's victories in the Persian wars. In ancient times this had already been holy ground: cyclopean walls, nearby but not shown, belong to a much earlier sanctuary.

The temple opposite was built over the tomb of Erechtheus, the legendary king from whom Athens claimed descent, who was identified with Poseidon himself. Columns carved in living forms make this portico of the caryatids one of the jewels of Attic art.

96   *Opposite:* Erechtheum, Athens. *Fritz Henle*

Theseum, Athens   *Mella*

On the hill above the Agora, Athens' busy civic center, stands the Theseum, or temple of Hephaestus *(above)*. This remarkably preserved shrine to the patron deity of the metalworkers became in Christian times the church of Saint George—and with this conversion came its great, covering barrel vault.

Opposite: Roman temple of Jupiter, Athens. *Kostich*

Rome

If Rome cannot boast of a building comparable to the Parthenon, it can state its own solid contributions: a genius for creating urban dignity. The Forum *(opposite)* was the city's religious and political center. Near the three columns that remain of its temple of Castor and Pollux, Caesar's body was cremated. Beyond, in the temple of Vesta, was the Sacred Fire tended by the Vestal Virgins.

Ruined colonnades, such as those remaining at Byblos *(right)*, remind us of the imperial hand of Rome: diversity and uniformity are neatly balanced, and importance is gained by means of superb civic planning.

Roman colonnade, Byblos

Temple of Jupiter, Baalbek   *Photos: Mella*

The Jupiter Elagabalus honored by the Romans had long been worshiped as Baal by the inhabitants of the Lebanese city of Baalbek; the towering columns of the temple *(right)* rest on gigantic stones.

The Pantheon, Rome   *Hürlimann*

Since Hadrian, called the most gifted amateur architect among the Emperors, designed
the Pantheon *(above)*, his inscription attributing the building to Agrippa has been
described as a sign of his "mock modesty." The Pantheon has long been famous as the
oldest (110–125 A.D.) roofed building still standing intact; now it is further valued as
the monument to what Paul MacKendrick calls "the liberation of religious architecture
from the Greek tyranny of the rectangular box" which the Roman invention of poured
concrete made possible. Nor is it haunted by the myriad deities of Rome to whom it was
dedicated—gods whose tenure was already doomed. Rather it engages by its enduring
nonreligious qualities. "Euclid alone has looked on beauty bare," Edna St. Vincent
Millay sang, and so, too, Hadrian must have felt when, as an exercise in geometrical
abstractions, he sought to give spatial expression to the interplay of the square and the
circle.

JUDAISM The basic difference between the sacred monuments of the ancient Near East and the holy edifices of the living religions which originated there did not prevent the Jews, Christians, and Moslems from using sites sacred to the gods and goddesses of antiquity. On the rocky outcropping atop Mount Moriah in Jerusalem now stands the Dome of the Rock, the oldest existing mosque; built in the seventh century, it encloses the exact spot from which, according to Islamic tradition, the Prophet Mohammed took off on his famous night journey to heaven. Three centuries earlier, a Christian pilgrim mentioned visiting the site; and archaeology reveals that the Christians must have torn down the sanctuary dedicated to Jupiter Capitolinus which the Romans had erected in the second century. This, in turn, had replaced the Great Temple of the Jews first built in the reign of Solomon, about 960 B.C., and finally leveled by the Roman armies in 70 A.D. Still earlier, when Jerusalem, or Jebus, was the stronghold of the Jebusites, the naked rock itself was the Altar of the Burnt Offering; examination of the cave under the rock shows an aperture through which the sacrificial blood trickled into the cave.

The religions of the ancient Near East were state religions: the rulers derived their political power from the gods to whom they belonged; the myths explained the relationship, and the official cult was concerned with renewing it. In Egypt, the pharaoh-god linked the human and divine worlds. In Mesopotamia, although the kings were human, they were the earthly stewards of the divinity to whom the city belonged: at Babylon, the king carried Marduk's insignia at the solemn New Year's Festival in which the god's primeval victory over the powers of chaos was re-enacted. The ceremonies of both regions aimed at securing for the vulnerable human community cosmic favor and stability, a concept reflected in the design of their sacred monuments.

The builders of the mighty temple complexes of antiquity were concerned primarily with the exteriors. They lavished their art on the façade of the cult building; the rest of the buildings within the temple enclosure might be plain and unassuming. Within the courtyard and before the imposing sanctuary were the sacrificial altars, where the ceremonies were staged. The holy of holies, entered only by the king and priests, was a box-like room, dimly lit, just large enough to accommodate the divine image and the treasures dedicated to the divinity. Interior space was designed, as in the pyramids, to be the golden needle hidden in the stone haystack, or, as in the Parthenon, for what C. R. Morey calls "the proper relief and isolation of the colonnade of the porch."

Very different in their essential requirements are the synagogues, churches, and mosques, we know, in which interior space, scaled to the size of the congregation, is the primary factor. At the time King Solomon had the Great Temple built, the Jewish temple resembled those of other state religions, even though the Jews had already set themselves apart from the religious systems of the kingdoms around them, which were rigidly hieratical and obsessed with ritual, preoccupied with man's relationship to the divinities immanent in nature. The Jews conceived of their God as transcending concrete phenomena. They were party to a covenant which, interpreted and extended by a series of "rhapsodic" prophets, made each individual an equal partner in the pact with God. The Covenant was not destroyed with the Temple nor could it be evaded by exile from the homeland.

"By the waters of Babylon, there we sat down; yea, we wept when we remembered Zion." So the uprooted and enslaved Jews in their Babylonian exile, 586–539 B.C., gathered together for strength and comfort. Then the priests, their sacerdotal duties having vanished with the destruction of their temple, became scribes and conscientiously started compiling and writing their people's oral traditions, customs, and laws so that every man might read how the covenants God made with successive tribal patriarchs became, through Moses, *the* Covenant. A new kind of worship resulted. Guided by the Commandments and strengthened by the prophets' poetic sermons, the gatherings of individuals joined by a common faith, misery, and hope and filled with an intense homesickness, at first spontaneous and unregularized, slowly became routine and traditional. Thus the concept of the congregation gradually took form.

It was ready at hand when an utterly different form of worship was introduced and sanctioned by Ezra, "the priest and scribe of the law of the God of heaven," on his arrival in Jerusalem, about 400 B.C. He had come from Babylon to revive, reorganize, and reform the Jewish community, the descendants of those who had eagerly retraced the eight hundred miles separating them from their homeland when Cyrus, King of Persia, issued his edict of liberation in 538 B.C. The Judaea they found was a land ravaged and poverty-stricken. Despair had dampened their zeal and apathy their will. To them Ezra brought not only the finished Pentateuch, much as it is today, but also spiritual direction and energy. Standing on a simple wooden platform, flanked by scribes—not priests but men of the people respected for their learning and wisdom, the Men of the Great Synagogue—Ezra read to the entire population the Law of Moses as it had been set down in writing, a body of laws based on the ethic of a society of free men possessed of equal rights and obligations. He also explained the meaning of each part, and pointed out its application. This was the service.

Inevitably this made it obligatory for every believer to learn to read, that he might himself study and interpret the Torah and participate in the communal life. A literate people made it possible for the Torah to replace the Temple as the religious authority; the hand-written scrolls, available to all, were housed in the Ark, which in the days of the Temple's pre-eminence had rested in the guarded holy of holies. With the growth of the synagogue the priests ceased to be officials of a cult; they became trustees of the sacred worth of the Torah and of the vast body of traditions which governed the secular as well as the sacred aspects of the life of the congregation.

The synagogue, from the Greek word meaning "assembly," was in spirit and practice the very opposite of the ancient Near Eastern temple. Formed by the genius and history of the Jews, it was a unique creation. And when, five hundred years after Ezra had sanctioned the congregational service and given the people the Torah, the Temple which had been rebuilt under his leadership was again despoiled and razed by the Romans and the Jews were again scattered in alien communities, they possessed the institution whereby they could maintain their cohesion and continuance. Wherever they went, the Torah went with them and made a holy place of whatever room the congregation met in.

A congregation requires interior space, but the building enclosing the space can have any style and be made of any material. Because the Jews were originally nomads they never developed an architectural style: Solomon's Temple, fashioned by Canaanite builders and artisans, was Canaanite in tradition and idiom, and the synagogues, scattered far and wide, resembled other buildings in the area in which they were set. They were seldom of great size, for this would have defeated the synagogue's primary purpose, that is to be a well-lighted place where men could meet for study and hear the rabbi's religious interpretations. The rabbi was not a priest, but a "master," in the sense of a teacher in a religious classroom where each member was expected to participate in the lesson and discussion. Only thus does the synagogue fulfill the fundamental Jewish conception of study as a mode of worship. The center of both religious worship and religious learning, the synagogue existed wherever there was a community of Jews, and its Torah gave them, in Heine's words, a "portable fatherland." This dual role of the synagogue was adopted by Judaism's two great offshoots, Christianity and Islam.

The Ark from a synagogue, Dura-Europos *Mella*

According to the Talmud, wherever ten adult male Jews—a *minyan*—live, a synagogue must be founded. It can be in a private dwelling. The room at left was in a house that served as a synagogue in the important Roman commercial center of Dura-Europos, on the bank of the Euphrates; hidden by the desert for seventeen hundred years, this town was preserved intact after the Roman garrison evacuated it about 240 A.D.

Over the Ark, where the scrolls of the Law are housed, Solomon's Temple appears, its ancient splendor stated in the architectural language of the Roman Empire. The lively Old Testament scenes flanking it—Solomon sitting in judgment, and Joseph amid his brethren—reveal that the commandment against graven images was not interpreted strictly until later.

The white limestone of the third-century Hellenistic synagogue at Capernaum *(opposite)* was enhanced by its setting in the midst of houses constructed of black lava blocks. A main hall, about 80 feet long and 60 feet wide, opened, on its east side, onto a colonnaded court. The stone carvings indicate the rich decoration; the walls may have been covered with frescoes.

In the Middle Ages, when Spain was the center of Jewish life and Jewish scholars were instrumental in introducing science to Western Europe, Toledo, the heart of this flowering, had nine synagogues and five Talmudic academies. Of all, only the Tránsito *(right)* and Santa Maria la Blanca, so renamed when taken from the Jews and made into a church in 1411, still stand as reminders of this great past.

The Synagoga del Tránsito was built in 1356–1357 for the use of Samuel haLevi Abulaffia, treasurer to and victim of Pedro the Cruel; it remained a Jewish house of instruction and worship until the expulsion of the Jews in 1492. Later it was consecrated as a church to the "transition" of the Virgin—hence its peculiar name. It is the finest and purest example of *Mudejar* art, that wonderful compound of Oriental arabesques and Syrian acanthus leaves; in an exquisite, often-copied Hebrew script, psalms and Biblical passages are carved in a continuous frieze around the interior.

Upon their expulsion from Spain, many of the Spanish, or Sephardic, Jews went to Venice, where a community of Jews from the Levant and Germany was already established. Despite objections from the Inquisition, the Sephardim were welcomed in Venice, to which their overseas trading brought prosperity.

Joseph Pardo, a respected Talmudic scholar of Venice, was invited to become the first rabbi of the Amsterdam synagogue—Amsterdam soon to be called the Venice of the north.

Synagoga del Tránsito, Toledo   *Mella*

Levantine synagogue, Venice   *Yivo*

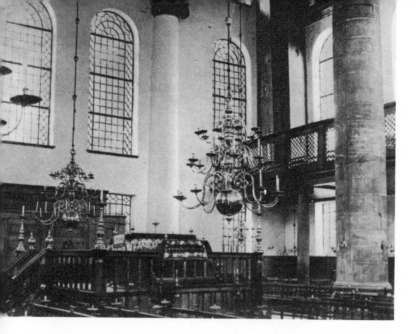

Sephardic synagogue,
the so-called
"Portuguese,"
Amsterdam, 1675

Below: Rotterdam
synagogue, destroyed
by German bombs,
May 14, 1940

The Marranos, Spanish Jews who remained true to
Judaism despite their baptism as Christians, settled
in Amsterdam shortly after 1600. Their services,
held in secret, made them suspect to the Holland-
ers, struggling against Spain and Catholicism, and
when the Jews congregated in their private synagogue on the Day of Atonement the authorities
were convinced that conspiracy was afoot. The
synagogue was raided and the congregation jailed.
Fortunately, one of the Jewish leaders spoke Latin,
and was able to assure the Dutch that his party
were not Papists but victims of the Inquisition;
he also pointed out the commercial advantages the
Marranos would bring to the port. The Dutch permitted the Yom Kippur services to continue, and
soon the position of the refugees was regularized.

By the time the stately Sephardic synagogue
shown above was built, Amsterdam had a population of more than four thousand Jews and had become the capital of European Jewry.

The wealth and elegance of the Rotterdam community expressed itself in the synagogue at right,
which, like others erected in Western and Central
Europe, followed the prevailing architectural style.

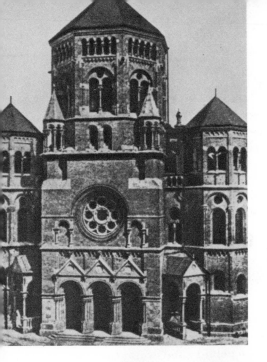

Synagogue, Munich

The medieval synagogues at Worms, 1180, and Regensburg, 1227, each had its two-nave hall and vaulted ceiling. These were built during the centuries when the liturgical forms of the Jewish service were becoming crystallized.

The impressive Romanesque building at left, the main Jewish synagogue in Munich, housed the sizable Jewish population long resident in Bavaria. It was among the first of the German synagogues to be defiled and destroyed by the Nazis.

Old Jewish Synagogue, and (at right) Jewish Town Hall, Prague

Photos: Yivo

In many cities, such as Prague, the Jews had their own community government that dealt with the non-Jewish governmental offices. The office of the Exilarch, who had been the recognized leader of the Jews in their Babylonian captivity, was continued into modern times, in European Jewish centers, in the role of the civic-religious leaders of the communities. These communities maintained their own schools and social services, internal jurisdiction, and systems of taxation.

Sometimes the Jews were confined within ghettos; sometimes, as in Italian cities such as Pisa and Leghorn, there was a community but no ghetto. (In Leghorn, the communal services operated through societies, and there were societies to cover every need, even one for "Dowering Poor Brides"!)

109

House of Study, Miedzyboz — *Yivo*

This modest and simple House of Study *(Beth-hamidrash)* in Miedzyboz, U.S.S.R., belonged to the Baal Shem-Tov, the founder of modern Hasidism. *Baal Shem-Tov* means in Hebrew "Master of the Good Name." Jew and Christian, Polish nobility and peasant, came to this man for what were said to be miraculous cures.

Hasidism follows the path of emotional exaltation, the ecstatic approach to God. The Baal Shem-Tov taught that man comes nearest to God not in sorrow but in joy. Despair, a consequence of sin, can be cured by true repentance; therefore, eat, drink, dance, and come close to God; the Lord will heed the happy prayers of the unlettered as surely as He does the serious utterances of the learned. Even for the Hasidim, however, study of the Bible and Talmud remained a part of worship, and each community, no matter how poor, set aside a place for it. This one-room house, built about 1750, was dignified as an academy and library and was truly a place made holy to the word of God.

Wooden Synagogues

By the eighteenth century, the greatest concentration of Jews was in Eastern Europe. For those scattered in Poland's cities, towns, and villages, the synagogue was the home of their souls and the center of their communal life. Crowded into ghettos or living poorly in rural districts, fearing the violence periodically directed against them, these people made their synagogues the witness to their glowing faith and devotion to God. The buildings are ashes now—like the millions who worshiped in them. Not one synagogue escaped. Of the great number in Eastern Europe, we possess only pictures, such as those on this and the following two pages, from the files of the Institute of Polish Architecture which, long before the Nazis defiled Poland, studied these synagogues.

The ancient synagogue had served solely as a prayer hall for the men. Its focal point was the Ark, covered by its curtain, *parocheth*. Before this altar-cupboard, which contained the scrolls on which the Torah was written, was a landing, approached by a flight of steps and enclosed by a balustrade, where the ritual of the showing of the Torah was performed. On either side of the steps were the candlesticks, the menorahs—also the desk, the *amid*, used by the cantor, and the *bima*, the platform from which the Torah

was read and the lectures and instructions delivered. Later, a gallery for the women was added, and a vestibule that gave protection from the elements and served as the assembly room for the Council of Elders, the Kahal. The first recorded prayer room for women was added to the synagogue at Worms in the thirteenth century.

The location of the *bima* was not prescribed by ritual, since it was associated largely with secular matters; it was customarily relegated to the middle of the synagogue, whose dim light made it a place to be avoided by men intent on reading and studying. As new conditions made the synagogue the center for the Jewish community's secular affairs (it was sometimes even the jail), the *bima* gained in use and importance. About the seventeenth century, a new floor plan made its appearance: the main hall became a square, with each of its four walls divided into three identical bays. The Ark was always placed in the middle of the east wall, and the *bima* occupied the position marked off by the four central pillars. Hasidic rabbis, no longer merely teachers, mounted the *bima* to advise and admonish their followers. Given a canopy and finally a cupola with a place for a lantern inside, this platform became the very heart of the building.

Bima in Przedbórz synagogue

In the early eighteenth-century synagogue at Mohylew, Poland *(above)*, we see the two entrances – the lower for the men, the upper for women. At Felsztyn, the interior of the synagogue *(left)*, which dates from the end of the eighteenth or beginning of the nineteenth century, was covered with polychrome paintings.

The intricately decorated interior of the synagogue at Przedbórz, built about 1760 *(right)*, was in contrast with its plain, unobtrusive exterior *(overleaf, top left)*.

Synagogue at Przedbórz

Synagogue at Ostropol

Its tiered roof gave the synagogue at Ostropol *(above, right)*, dating probably from the seventeenth century, a pagoda-like air. The main hall was surrounded by a cluster of annexes, each with its own roof.

Synagogue at Jurborg, latter half of eighteenth century

The synagogue at Wolpa *(right)*, probably early eighteenth century, shows the skillful and artistic construction of the lofty interior vaulting over the *bima*. The lower structures accommodated a vestibule on the west side and prayer rooms for women along the north and south walls. It seems to have been customary to make the floor of the main hall three steps below that of the vestibule. A gallery on the west wall, reached by a steep flight of steps, was probably for school-children; from there they could see the Ark and follow the service.

Interior vaulting, synagogue at Wolpa

112

Synagogue at Ostrog　　　　　　　　　*Photos: Yivo*

Stone Synagogues

Above we see the rear of the synagogue at Ostrog, U.S.S.R. (formerly Poland), with its impressive stone fortress. A subterranean passage led from the synagogue to the round tower of an old castle, through which messengers were sent for help in time of need.

The large synagogue at Będzin, Poland *(left)*, was typical of many in Eastern Europe built of stone and brick. It dominated the skyline of the Jewish quarters which surrounded it, as the castle dominated the town's skyline.

Synagogue at Będzin

Paradesi synagogue, Cochin

The Ark and *bima* in the beautiful Paradesi synagogue in Cochin, India *(left)*, serve a congregation that has been there since Roman times, when this part of the Malabar coast was the source of Rome's important pepper trade with India.

At the synagogue in Cairo *(overleaf)* tiled steps lead to the curtained Ark. Before it is the *bima* as it was in the older churches—a platform for honoring a member of the congregation who was asked to read from the Torah, and a place for simple announcements. It had no feature to rival the architectural importance of the Ark.

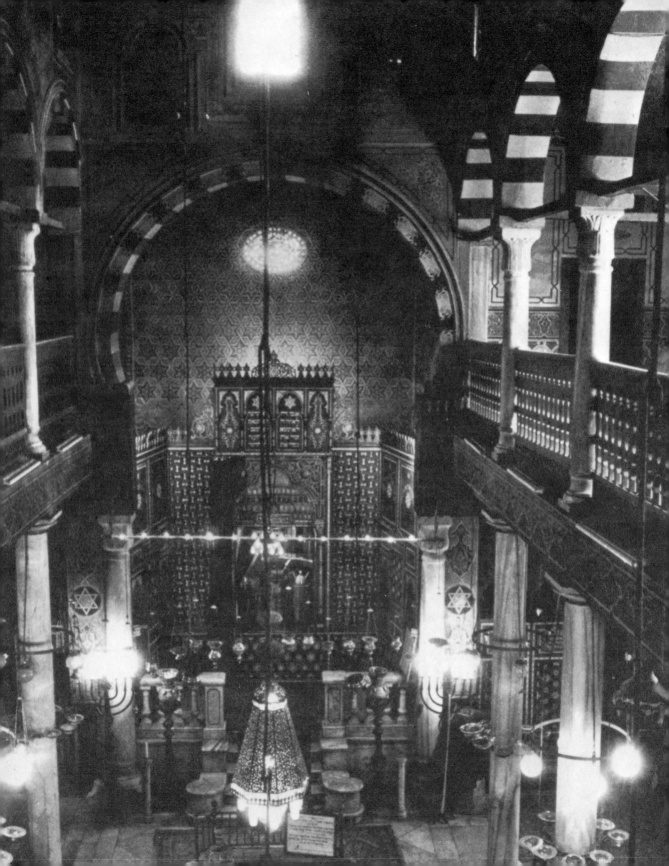

Modern Synagogues

Today the term synagogue is rarely given to a new building; it is usually a temple (with an identifying Hebrew name), and it may serve an orthodox, conservative, or reformed congregation. The Jewish religious edifices constructed in the last century and the first third of this century were essentially sanctuaries, housing the holy space where religious services were held; now they are being designed with additional space for a wide range of social, cultural, and philanthropic activities. They are, therefore, as many of them rightly call themselves, Jewish community centers.

As the synagogue was the outcome of the Babylonian captivity and the reading of the Torah was the fruit of Ezra's teaching, so the synagogue's association with the Jewish community center came into being when Jewish groups were set apart by their faith from the Christian or Moslem majority around them. When Jews were forced to live in ghettos, they maintained their own civil administration (governing according to Talmudic law) and dealt with the authorities as a group. At other times, when they were not so confined, they still maintained their religious and cultural identity and cared for their own social needs and well-being. Thus it came about that synagogue and "town hall" were housed either in the same building or in adjacent ones. Religious life and community life were intertwined.

The contemporary emphasis is in the nature of a return to this earlier association, out of a desire to share in and identify with a heritage. So pronounced is this desire that older temples, built for religious activities, are adding a community center for social and cultural activities. In this respect, the Jewish communities share the same impulse that animates the religious building of other faiths.

Since the Jews never developed their own architectural style, their modern temples and Jewish community centers are being built, as were those of the Middle Ages, in the idiom of the times.

Opposite: Synagogue, Cairo. *Elisofon*

Temple Mishkan Tefila, Chestnut Hill, Massachusetts
Dennis Stock/Magnum Photos

Temple Beth El, Providence, Rhode Island

Temple Beth Abraham, Tarrytown, New York

Temple Beth Sholom, Miami Beach, Florida

ISLAM Islam was born of the desert and formed by the nomads. When the followers of Mohammed looked beyond their Arabian cradleland in the seventh century, they had only the crudest architectural notions and most rudimentary building skills. The Kaaba, principal sanctuary of the Prophet's tribe, and the sacred well of Zamzam lay within a small, oblong, rock-walled enclosure which separated them from the simple mud-brick houses of Mecca that pressed around them. Yet within a century after Mohammed's death (632 A.D.) his followers ruled the lands from Spain to Persia, and every town and settlement had its mosque.

Mohammed had taught that God was everywhere, and the Arabs customarily described a desert or empty space as having "nothing there but the presence of Allah." Islam never tolerated altars, images, or sacred relics and had no priests to officiate as intermediaries between man and God, but the mosque nevertheless played a vital part in the rules laid down for the believer's spiritual health. *Islam*—the word itself—means submission: submission to God's inscrutable will as it was revealed to Mohammed. Set forth in the Holy Koran are the five religious practices which God expects the faithful to observe.

Five times each day all Moslems are required to pray. At sunrise they are awakened by a voice, its long-drawn-out call sent in the four directions, repeating the confessions of faith and exhorting them to pray: "God is most great. I testify there is no god but one. I testify that Mohammed is the Prophet of God. Come to prayer. Come to salvation. Prayer is better than sleep. God is most great."

At noon, in the early afternoon, at sunset, and after the fall of darkness, the same call (minus the reference to sleep) is cried aloud for all to hear and heed. Every believer, whether he lives in a town or in the desert, whether he is traveling overland or across the sea, working in the field or shop, turns toward Mecca and says the *Fatiha*, which praises God, the Compassionate and Merciful, and seeks divine help and divine grace. While reciting the *Fatiha*—and, if he chooses, any additional verses from the Holy Koran—he bows and prostrates himself, touching the earth with his forehead; then he says the creed, the Moslem confession of faith: "There is no god but God and Mohammed is the Prophet of God."

At the noon prayer on Fridays (the holy day) the faithful praise God and make their confession of faith collectively in a mosque. There, under the direction of an *imam*—not a priest or holy man, but a leader chosen for his respected age or deep learning—the congregation recites the words and makes the prostrations in unison. The remaining reli-

Opposite: The Great Mosque of Samarra, near Baghdad, about 850. *Mella*

gious duties, which, with these, constitute the "Five Pillars" of Islam, govern almsgiving, fasting, and making the pilgrimage to Mecca.

The mosque need not be an edifice. (The word, from the Arabic *masjid*, suggests "a place of prostration," as *jami*, the other term used, means "a gathering place.") Only a space, enclosed to give unity, with an indication of the *qibla*, the direction of Mecca, is essential. Such a place is considered sacred, since the Moslems observe God's command to Moses: "Put off thy shoes from off thy feet, for the place whereon thou standest is holy ground." So simple a concept for a place of holy worship was consonant with the "architectural vacuum" of Arab culture—Mohammed himself is said to have remarked: "The most unprofitable thing that eateth up the wealth of a Believer is building." But this primitive concept did not satisfy the Arabs when, in less than a generation after the Prophet's death, they had occupied places where the creative genius of many peoples had produced over long millennia rich and complex civilizations.

Their holy wars made the Arabs masters of regions dominated by two distinct cultural traditions. In the west, those groups who overran Palestine, Egypt, and Syria found themselves in a world where Hellenistic art and architecture had a thousand-year history, a world whose craftsmen built splendid cut-stone churches for imperial Byzantium as their forebears had built splendid pagan temples for imperial Rome. Even before them, and already skilled, the Phoenicians had formed their beehive *tholoi;* and, still earlier, the Egyptians had erected temples and tombs for the divine pharaohs. Here, at first, the Moslems merely appropriated the churches, either evicting the Christians outright or, as often happened, dividing the space—half church, half mosque.

The Arab groups who fanned out eastward into Mesopotamia and beyond came to the region where the predominant influence was Persian. Here they brought to an end the native Sassanid dynasty whose kings had revived the arts and glory of the ancient Persian empire; whose daring architects, virtuosi in exploring the potentials of brick construction, had erected royal residences with wide central halls where ovoid vaulted ceilings swept up to breathtaking heights. The impressive, lavishly decorated Sassanid style had replaced the earlier imperial audience halls where row upon row of lofty columns supported an expanse of flat roof. The first mosques built in the east have disappeared. In the remains of palaces—both Sassanid and ancient Persian—experts have found the architectural traditions and styles which the native workers used when, conscripted by their new Arab masters, they built their mosques.

It was this dependence of the Arabs on the conquered peoples to supply them with master builders and craftsmen (the Greeks in Syria, the Persians in Iraq and Iran, and the Copts in Egypt) that produced Islamic architecture, a richly textured amalgam of many styles and techniques. Its development belongs to the larger story of the rise of Islamic civilization: having once imposed their religion, the Arabs respected the arts and sciences of the peoples they ruled and, learning from them, stamped with their own genius the beauty and knowledge they had inherited.

The Kaaba, or "Navel of the World," the House of Abraham at Mecca, part of which is shown below, is to Moslems the Holy of Holies, an altar whose sanctity began with man and is everlasting. At God's command, Abraham himself—counted the first of the prophets and the founder of Islam—built the immense cube of basalt blocks that stands 34 feet high, 31 feet wide, and 38 feet long. Embedded in its southeast corner, about five feet above the base, is the Black Stone which fell from heaven in Adam's time.

Mecca, the birthplace of Mohammed, had religious and cultic significance for the tribes who wandered in Arabia even before the Prophet's birth, about 570. Moslems face toward Mecca when they pray because Mohammed commanded it; but the pilgrimage he enjoined the faithful to make, if possible, once in their lives, celebrates events and sites of pre-Islamic traditions which the Prophet associated with Hebrew legends. Thus, the miraculous well of Zamzam (at left, below) is believed to be the spring God revealed to Hagar so that Ishmael, the son she had borne to Abraham, might not perish. It is Ishmael from whom the Arabs claim descent.

Entering the Great Mosque through the Gate of Salvation—one of its nineteen gates—and passing through the inner Gate of the Sons of the Old Woman, the pilgrim salutes the shrine. "Here am I, O God, at Thy Command. Thou hast no equal. Here am I." The pilgrim must circle the Kaaba in the ancient rite of circumambulation three times: on his arrival, when he returns from the day-long ceremony of the stoning at Mina (the reenactment of Ishmael's driving the Devil away), and at his ceremonial farewell.

The Kaaba, Mecca   *Paul Popper Ltd.*

Mosques of the Umayyad Dynasty, 661–750

The Dome of the Rock *(right)*, at Jerusalem, is the oldest existing Moslem-built religious edifice. Its site, on the Sakkara, the name given the rocky outcropping which forms the summit of Mount Moriah, is doubly hallowed, for here David had his altar and Solomon his Temple; from here, astride Buraq, the fabulous winged horse with a woman's head and peacock's tail, Mohammed took off on his miraculous, quick-as-a-flash night journey to heaven.

Caliph Abd al-Malik, who built the Dome of the Rock in 691, designed it as a "Place of Witness" which he hoped would rival Constantine's Church of the Holy Sepulchre. In doing so he gave us the finest example of the rotunda-type building in Byzantine architecture. Between the Rock, encircled with a marble colonnade and crowned with a mighty, serene dome, and the outer octagonally shaped wall is the processional space in which pilgrims circumambulate.

To be assured of success in this venture, by which he meant not only to glorify his faith but to proclaim his political power, Abd al-Malik conscripted great numbers of skilled artisans from regions as far away as Persia and appropriated whatever would enhance the new shrine—for example, the magnificent copper gilt dome brought from a church in Baalbek. The building was restored about 825.

The Dome of the Rock, Jerusalem   *Alinari*

The Aqsa mosque *(below, left)*, near the Dome of the Rock on the Sakkara, has suffered frequent damage from earthquakes, and has often been rebuilt. Creswell dates much of the present structure from repairs and additions made by Caliph al-Zahir, about 1035.

This mosque originated as a place of prostration improvised amid the ruins of Herod's Stoa, destroyed by Titus in 70 A.D. "The Saracens," wrote the European pilgrim Arculf, who visited the Holy Land in 670, "now frequent a quadrangular place of prayer, which they have built rudely, constructing it by setting great beams on some remains of ruins: this house can, it is said, hold three thousand men at once."

Aqsa mosque, Jerusalem   *Mella*

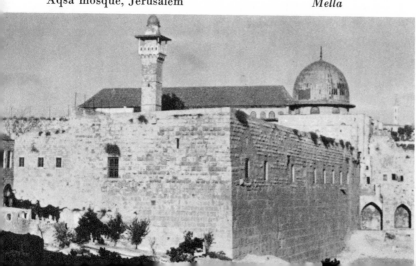

Under the patronage of the Umayyads artists, skilled craftsmen, and merchants were attracted to the court; Damascus became a metropolis. The Caliph Walid decided to provide a mosque larger and fairer than any church. He appropriated the site of the Cathedral of Saint John, originally a magnificent Roman temple dedicated to Jupiter which had become a Christian basilica when the Emperor Theodosius, who reigned from 379 to 395, forbade all pagan ceremonies. The cathedral took its name from the legend that the head of Saint John rested under the domed shrine.

In the Great Mosque *(below)* the pagan elements—temple, temenos, and tower—were given an organic unity. The immense trapezoidal temenos, the temple's sacred ground, became the great court enclosed by a noble arched colonnade. The solitary tower, tall and square, acquired a slim steeple and became a minaret, the first to be used in Islamic architecture.

The interior walls of the mosque glowed with golden murals and mosaics lighted by six hundred lamps hung by golden chains from the ceiling. Traces remain of a mosaic landscape, probably the largest ever made in a building; in it, with consummate skill and charm, the artists delineated the city's crowded buildings, bridges, and tree-lined river. Arab travelers who saw the mosque before wars and fires scarred its splendor counted it one of the wonders of the world. It inspired many other famous mosques, notably that of Córdoba.

The Great Mosque, also called the Great Umayyad Mosque, at Damascus, 705–715; the oldest congregational mosque in continuous use   *Mella*

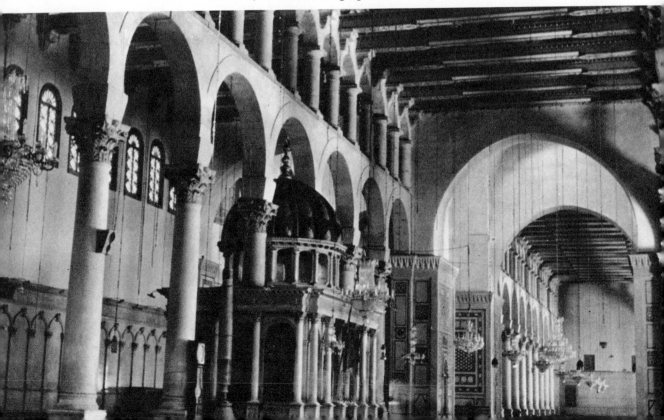

Abd-ar-Rahman was the sole survivor of the Umayyads when the Abassid caliphate was proclaimed in 750; he escaped to Spain, a distant outpost of the Moslem empire, and founded the emirate of Córdoba in 756. He is remembered for having begun, in 788, the Great Mosque at Córdoba *(right)*, still one of the most strikingly beautiful sacred monuments in the Spanish world.

His mosque incorporated the large church of Saint Vincent, built by the Visigoths on the site of a Roman temple to Janus. Constructed in the Syrian style by Syrian refugees who followed him to Spain, the Great Mosque is called "Moorish." (The Christians made no fine distinctions among the Berbers, Syrians, and Copts who triumphantly carried Islam into Spain, but called them all men from Morocco—"Moors.") Successive emirs enlarged and beautified the mosque until, when it was finished, about 1000, it ranked as the third largest in the world.

After Córdoba was taken by the Christians in 1236 the mosque served for three hundred years as a cathedral. The principal change made was to brick up the openings which permitted the aisles to flow into the court, leaving only a central doorway. But time and differences in customs also affected the mosque. Thus, the fountains in the outer court—where the faithful obeyed the command to wash hands, face, neck, and feet, and to rinse out mouth and nostrils before entering the mosque—were allowed to fall into disrepair. (And, when the same neglect blighted the hundreds of public baths in the city, the Moslems were quite convinced that Christians, on whom water was sprinkled at baptism, never bathed thereafter.)

The Great Mosque was not seriously tampered with until 1523, when Charles V permitted a new chapel to be built in its very midst. When he visited Córdoba and saw where the clergy had placed their chapel, he said, "If I had known what you wished to do, you would not have done it, because what you are carrying out there is to be found everywhere, and what you had formerly does not exist anywhere else in the world."

Ibn-Tulun mosque of I-Maydan, 876–879   *Mella*

The Great Mosque, Córdoba, Spain, 788–1000

Mosques of the Abassid Dynasty, 750–1258

When the Abassids moved the caliphate from Damascus to Baghdad in 762, Islamic architecture was enriched by idioms foreign to the Hellenistic tradition and expressive of the vigorous mental and artistic impulses of Persia, as well as of the religious concepts of the long-dead Mesopotamian cities.

In the west, the temenos had inspired open, spreading courts; in the east, the ancient enclosure became the *ziyada*, an outer walled-in area with fountains framing the temple. The Persians built in brick, coating the surfaces with fine and hard white stucco which also outlined the arches, lightened the long roof-line, and provided a lacy grillwork for the windows. They continued to use the Sassanid vault that soared up from the ground; it became the familiar *iwan*.

All the mosques built when Baghdad was in its glory vanished when the Mongols leveled the city in 1285. But from the impressive ruins nearby of the Great Mosque of Samarra *(shown on page 116)* we know that the Abassids added their own affection for the grandiose. Samarra, whose swirling minaret, long voiceless, still stands, was built so that its huge bastioned walls, 784 feet by 512 feet, would contain the caliph's sixty thousand soldiers at their Friday prayers.

THE IBN-TULUN mosque *(opposite page, left)*, of noble simplicity with a high-swirling Samarra-type minaret, was built in the ninth century at al-Fustat, then the capital of Egypt. When the Fatimids conquered the Nile Valley, they built a new capital called al-Qahirah, "The Triumphant," from which comes its present name, Cairo. The mosque of Ibn-Tulun was neglected, frequented only by Mecca-bound pilgrims, who used it as a campsite. Vast and deserted, it provided a perfect hiding place for Husam ad-Din Lajin, murderer of the sultan Khalil. Undetected, he lived there while rallying his supporters to gain the throne; in gratitude he restored the mosque in 1296 and endowed it.

The Golden Mosque of Khadumain, Baghdad   *Mella*   Imam Riza shrine, Meshed

Mosques of the Shi'a Sect

The Shi'a sect is the main deviation from the Sunna, as Islamic orthodoxy is called. Shi'a means the "party of Ali," that is, Mohammed's son-in-law and the leaders, Imams, of his house. Shi'a is a word telescoping events long past with messianic expectations in the future. The chief strength of the Shi'ites is in Iran.

The differences between Shi'a and Sunna stem from the issue of succession which first arose at the Prophet's death in 632. How was the secular leader of the Moslem community to be chosen? The Sunna, the traditionalists, believed in the tribal custom of elective succession, the Shi'a in hereditary succession – Mohammed's successor, *khalifa*, must come from his house. Their candidate was Ali, both a blood cousin of the Prophet and, through his marriage to Fatima, the Prophet's son-in-law. Moreover, Ali had been the very first to recognize Mohammed's divine mission and became his first convert.

Subsequently the Shi'ites accepted the idea that God selects their leader and thus makes him infallible; that in every age, in one man, the light of Mohammed shines; and that only their Imam's divine wisdom can interpret the Koran and the law which governs every act of a believer's life. They further believe that twelve Imams of Ali's house were living transmitters of God's will and word, and that this line of infallible leaders stopped when the twelfth one disappeared mysteriously about 878 – they point to a small hole in the Samarra mosque. A large group of Shi'ites in Iran holds that this

Paul Popper Ltd.　　　　The Golden Mosque of Fatima, Qum　　　　*Mella*

Twelfth Imam is the messiah, Mahdi, who, in a secret place, is awaiting the "end of the ages" to reappear and proclaim his rule of righteousness.

Differences within the Shi'a sect itself center on the number and identity of the Imams and which are to be specially venerated. Thus, the Isma'ili broke away from the Shi'a over the succession of the Seventh Imam. The Isma'ili have had a spectacular history since a young Persian Shi'ite, Hasan ibn-al-Sabbah, joined them in 1071. He is notorious as the first grand master of the Assassins, a corruption of *hashish*, the drug under whose influence his followers carried out his politics-by-murder. Two hundred years later the Mongols broke the Assassins' political power and leveled their mountain strongholds. Members of the last leader's family migrated south to India, where they lived quiet respectable lives. In 1866, before the High Court of Bombay, a descendant was able to trace his lineage back to Hasan ibn-al-Sabbah and establish his right to receive the tithe the once-accursed leader had imposed on his followers. This is the basis of the veneration accorded the Aga Khan and of his wealth.

Whether ruined or restored, the mosques of Iran set forth the qualities of the Persian genius: a poetry written in bright color and curving line, an instinct for elegance, and a love of the grand scale. Design and color were in the baked enameled brick applied over the immense spherical surfaces of these mosques in intricate cursive motifs – curving stems, delicate buds, leaves and flowers and holy words written in the angular, handsome Kufic style. The design, drawn to full size and brilliant color, was traced piece by piece on the smooth surface of a plaster bed – flat where the walls to be covered were flat and, for the dome, curved to its profile. Meanwhile the ceramists made hundreds of thousands of tiles of each color – turquoise, cobalt, the midnight blue of lapis lazuli, light emerald, yellows ranging from lightest cream to deepest saffron, pure white, and soot black. Workers cut the tiles to fit the design: the edge of each small bit was rubbed smooth and tapered from the glazed surface back to a narrow ridge. Finally the fragments were arranged, glazed side down, on the plaster bed and spread with a thick coat of plaster which, oozing through the spaces between the tapered edges, fixed the pieces firmly. Section by section the mosque was clothed in tile.

The marvelous mosque of Isfahan (*below and opposite*) is the culmination of the thousand-year union of Persian architecture and Islamic devotion; it marks, as Arthur Upham Pope says, "one of those perfect moments when power and elegance are in tranquil equilibrium."

Below and opposite: Masjid-i-Shah, Isfahan, 1616   *Photos: Mella*

Below: Blue or Sultan Ahmed Mosque, Istanbul   *Mella*

THE OTTOMAN EMPIRE, during its golden age under Sultan Suleiman the Magnificent, stretched from Gibraltar to Persia, and from Vienna to the southern tip of Arabia. Its heart was the great city which, when it had been called Constantinople, was second only to Jerusalem as Christendom's holy pilgrimage site. As Islambol, whence Istanbul, it was, after 1453, the City of Many Islams. Whether it was the capital of the Byzantine empire or of the Ottoman, its skyline was dominated by Justinian's Santa Sophia. Moslem architects copied its plan for their mosques, adding slender minarets—four for the mosque of Sultan Suleiman, 1550–1557, and six for the Blue, or Sultan Ahmed Mosque, 1616.

Cloisters of the Kutb mosque, Delhi   *Viollet*

THE MOSLEM CONQUEST of Delhi in 1192 saw the beginning of Islamic architecture in India. To create the mosque named for the conqueror, Kutb-ud-din, the Moslems in 1200 dismembered the largest and finest Hindu temples. Each of the mosque's pillars was formed out of two Hindu ones, one set above the other; in one mosque alone are more than a thousand pillars looted from fifty temples. Those in the cloisters of the Kutb mosque *(right)* are superb examples of eighth- and ninth-century Hindu carving.

The mosque *(above)* and palace *(below)* at Fatehpur Sikri   *Mella*

Fatehpur Sikri, complete with magnificent mosque and palace, was built by the emperor Akbar, between 1570 and 1585, and bears the signature of the Mogul dynasty that ruled northern India from 1526 to 1857. The site was soon deserted for lack of water.

The mosque's southern gateway *(above)*, dignified, noble, and jubilant with its crown of triple domes, rises 170 feet. The architects who designed its wide soaring arch, which frames a recessed semidome, created one of the world's monumental portals. On the other side of this gateway, the worshiper entered a court through a doorway scaled to human size. And within the court *(right)*, everywhere, the eye catches the echo of the domes.

130

Jamma Masjid mosque, Delhi *Mella / Cecil Beaton*

Shah Jahan, who created the Taj Mahal for love of his wife, also ordered his architects
to design at Delhi the immense and imposing Jamma Masjid mosque (*above*). Built in
1644–1658 of red sandstone and white marble, it has three gateways, noble stairs, slim
minarets, and great bulbous domes.

Islam crossed the Indian Ocean to the islands beyond; it is the main religion of Indonesia's millions, who worship in mosques such as this pagoda-like structure *(left)* at Djarnik, Sumatra.

Islam penetrated further into Asia. The huge colored brick mosque at Turfan *(below)* in Sinkiang province, China, dominates the landscape.

Hürlimann *Viollet*

Minarets

The landscape of Islam is rich in minarets. Eye-catching, the many silhouettes rising into the sky form seemingly endless variations on the theme of architectural height.

The theme itself was first stated by Mohammed when, at Medina, he was establishing the rituals of worship. He was seeking a distinctive way to mark the five times daily when the believers pray to God and profess their faith—seeking for a sound different from that of the *shofar* (the horn used by the Jews) and of the *naqus* (the wooden clapper which summoned Christians to church). One day, with this in mind, the Prophet sent his disciple Bilal, an Abyssinian, to the roof of his home to recite the creed and the call to prayer so that all Medina would hear. Bilal's sonorous voice saturated the still air and each syllable he slowly, solemnly intoned became part of the very atmosphere; the sound of a human voice magically enveloped the town, word after word drifting to earth from the height above. Thus the formal call to prayer, *adhan*, was introduced.

From *adhan*, the Arabic language formed *mu'adhdhin*, he who gives the call (the public crier), and *ma'dhana*, the place where the call is made. The English word "muezzin" approximates the equivalent *mu'adhdhin*; but strangely enough, minaret comes not from *ma'dhana*, but from *manara*, "a place where fire burns"—the Arabs' term for the Pharos, the famous lighthouse in Alexandria's harbor. Soon *manara* was applied to all lighthouses and, by extension, to all towers; inevitably it became a synonym for *ma'dhana*, the high tower of the mosque.

Minarets rise from Moslem communities from northwestern Africa eastward to Central Asia and, through Persia and India, to Malaya and Indonesia. More than three hundred and fifty million people submit to Islam's creed. In this religion, so coherent and uniform, the minarets seem to flaunt their individuality and diversity.

Below, left to right: Sultan-Hassa, Cairo. Mosque of Sheik Omar, Baghdad. Kutb Minar, Delhi, 238 feet high. Minaret at Isfahan.   *Photos: Mella*

VIII

CHRISTIANITY Church, as a word, has two meanings—the building used for Christian worship and the religious community of Christians—and therefore conveys how intimate is the connection between Christian architecture and the doctrine of fellowship with Christ and with the brethren. *Ecclesia*, a Greek word which gives the French their word *église*, was originally applied to the assembly of the freeborn citizens of the polis. The same term was used for the Jewish congregation, when the Scriptures were translated from Hebrew for the Greek-speaking, Hellenized Jews of Alexandria. Later, *ecclesia* described the Christian community. The very word can serve to remind us that Christianity, as both doctrine and edifice, began as a Jewish sect and grew to power in a Hellenistic world ruled by Rome.

Unfortunately, the earliest Christian churches have long since disappeared. Not one remains from the centuries when theology and liturgy, doctrine and organization were beginning to take form—the hazardous centuries during which hostile officials hounded and killed the Christians who refused to worship the emperor, and in which Christianity itself was fighting for its life against the Gnostic, Arian, and Monophysite heresies. Thus, we cannot know how the first churches differed from synagogues; we do know that in those early years Christianity remained within the Jewish fold. As Jesus Himself had remained within the Jewish Law, so did the Disciples He had chosen. Under James, first Bishop of Jerusalem, the congregations of the mother church were limited to Jews; non-Jews, such as the Greek Titus, had to be circumcised before they could be baptized. The Christians shared many practices, including baptism by immersion, with the Essenes, another Jewish sect; and like the Qumran Covenanters (known through the Dead Sea Scrolls), they held that only they among the chosen people of Israel were God's elect. Unlike the Jews, however, the Christians believed that in Jesus they beheld the Messiah (*Christos* is the Greek equivalent, meaning "he who is annointed") whose coming was to usher in the Kingdom of God. But this profound difference was not apparent to the Roman legions, who destroyed the Judaean churches along with all the synagogues and the Temple in Jerusalem in 70 A.D.

Neither do we know how those first Christian churches differed from the ones founded by Paul (who died about 67) in many cities around the Mediterranean. Paul felt that faith in the ministry, passion, and resurrection of Christ Jesus rendered the Jewish Law

Opposite: The Giralda minaret, transformed into the tower of the cathedral, Córdoba.

obsolete; breaking with the Mosaic tradition, he baptized Gentiles into the Christian community. The Disciples opposed this, but conflict over the inclusion of Gentiles ceased when, with the destruction of the mother church, the authority of Jerusalem was silenced.

Constantine's momentous Edict of Milan, in 313, and additional decrees granting Christians freedom of worship, transformed an unfashionable and seditious sect into a rich and powerful minority. Not only was the Church permitted to receive legacies; it was given state revenues, and decisions handed down by the episcopal courts, which heretofore had been respected solely within the Christian community, were declared to be legal and binding. The Christian community, though torn by differences of dogma, had developed an effective administrative organization; two hundred and fifty bishops, each attended by numerous presbyters and deacons, met at Nicaea in 325 for the Church's first council, to resolve, at the Emperor's command, their differences of doctrine.

The Christians started their great building of churches early in the fourth century. Eusebius of Caesarea, the father of ecclesiastical history, who died about 340, marveled at the flowering of new buildings—"Who can number the churches in every town?" The model the Christians adopted was the basilica, an important element in Roman architecture. The basilica, an integral part of the Forum complex, housed the law court and commercial center, and at its foot was the market where the people bought their food. It had never been tainted by association with pagan rituals but had been used only for secular activities. Its courts symbolized the stability and majesty of Roman law. In Rome, the basilica most admired, most imperial in size and ornamentation, was the one Trajan built about 112. It was 385 feet long and half as wide (the customary proportion), and its great length fronted on the Forum; its short ends curved to form apses. Its roof, sheathed in gilt bronze, was more splendid than the splendid Forum, which it stood above, at the head of three yellow marble steps. The marble interior was divided by 96 columns into an 87-foot-wide nave with double aisles. Against a cream-colored floor and walls veneered in fine white Carrara, the tinted marble of the columns created an Oriental opulence. It was this basilica that chiefly inspired the Christians in their building.

The Christian dogma teaches that the seed of the spiritual nature, implanted by baptism, is nourished by the body and blood of the divine Christ through participation in the Eucharist. The basilican church was the Eucharistic room. In its apse, oriented to the east, where formerly Roman judges had sat facing the litigants now the bishop and his presbyters and deacons sat facing the congregation; in the chancel or *cancelli* —as the Romans called the latticework balustrade that had separated the tribunal from the litigants and the public—the singers were installed; and between clergy and congregation was the altar, the place of sacrifice. Raised a few steps above the level of the nave, the altar represented the ancient, sacred, high place where God and man could meet. It was also the actual table, bare except for the chalice and paten, set for the Eucharistic banquet. Over the altar a canopy, the *ciborium*, proclaimed the table's special purpose and holiness. The basilica—that is, the church, in its architectural meaning—housed the congregation; and since the religious community of Christians thought of itself as the temple of the living God, as "the habitation of the Spirit; a spiritual house built of living stones," in effect the basilica housed the Church.

The other basic sacrament, baptism, by which the Christian is reborn in Christ, had its own building, the baptistry, near the entrance to the church at the western end of the basilica. The entrance might open on a space separated from the nave by a wall, or screen, or railing, to form a vestibule, the narthex; this was the place set aside for those who for one reason or another were not entitled to membership in the body of the congregation.

The site chosen for a basilican church was usually over the burial place of the saint to whom the church was dedicated, the building being so situated that the altar stood immediately above the venerated grave in the crypt. In these churches of early Christianity there was but one altar, and the Eucharist was a corporate act of concelebration. In the churches of San Paolo fuori le Mura (founded in 380, rebuilt on the original design in 1823), Santa Sabina (425), or Santa Maria Maggiore (432), all in Rome, the long columns flanking the nave still march in steady, emphatic rhythm toward the raised and canopied altar, and the great arch framing the eastern apse seems less a structural device than an arch of victory symbolizing the transition through death to life eternal.

In the course of the next five centuries a style we know as Romanesque evolved. The term, coined in 1819, is applied to churches displaying regional variations in the different areas of Western Europe while still relying on Roman building forms and techniques; each was groping to give architectural expression to individual changes in social conditions and religious temper. As distinctions between clergy and laity grew more rigid, little by little the sanctuary was rearranged—the bishop's throne was placed *between* the Eucharistic table and the congregation, the seats of the presbyters and deacons were removed, and the altar itself was pushed back against the east wall. (By the twelfth century, the candlesticks and cross, which formerly had been carried into the church when the liturgy started, adorned the altar.) The Eucharist, now generally called the "Mass," became a liturgical act performed by a priest assisted by a server; facing the altar with his back turned to the people, he said Mass on their behalf while they, from afar, witnessed a solemn ceremony. The east wall was further changed to meet the needs of the thousands of priests who, with the growing custom of saying Mass daily, required additional altars. Other innovations gradually affected the nave: as the veneration of saints and holy relics increased, for instance, the nave accommodated numerous shrines and, when an intense commiseration for Christ's Passion became an increasingly important part of the religious experience, the fourteen Stations of the Cross as well.

The churches in the Romanesque style were the creations of clerics well versed in architectural theory and of inspired master builders. Working together, experimenting, testing, and learning, they grew more daring and finally felt their way out of the inert stability of Roman construction to new principles of elasticity and equilibrium; using small dressed stones set in deep mortar, they realized in structures their noble visions of geometry.

Planners and artisans worked together to solve the most pressing problem, the need for additional altars. In the "radiating plan," which originated in France, the apse was circled by an ambulatory known as the *chevet*, from which a series of chapels radiated; in the "staggered plan," also French, the number of altars was increased by extending the aisles beyond the transepts to provide an apse at the end of each—and the transepts themselves might have apses, sometimes as many as three, set into their east walls. Transepts provided aesthetic relief from the monotony of the early basilican churches by forming new groupings which were rhythmically more interesting. The basilica was further modified by tall masonry shafts extending from floor to ceiling, which interrupted the solid longitudinal line of the galleries; the columns served to punctuate the aisles and form deep bays where shrines could nest.

The simple, flat wooden roof of the basilican church—so vulnerable to fire—was also modified. After the tenth century, the church builders made their vaults higher and wider, until a masonry ceiling, a hundred feet above the floor, might span a forty-foot-wide nave. Seen from the outside, a Romanesque church was a swelling but unified grouping, with the many-chapeled apse, the lofty-vaulted nave, and the transept with towers rising above the crossings. The stonecutters directed their artistry upon the exterior, ignored in the basilican church, and invested the capitals and portals with memorable sculpture.

By the latter part of the eleventh century some of the churches had begun to display the exciting vitality and virtuosity of Europe's hard-won self-assurance. (The greatest manifestation of that spirit, the First Crusade, began in 1096.) In the marvelous churches of the late Romanesque period—especially in those of France—we perceive the intimations of architectural grandeur to come.

Why was it France, and not Italy or Germany, that took the lead in creating Western Europe's only original architecture? Germany from the time of Charlemagne—who was crowned Holy Roman Emperor in Rome on Christmas Day, 800—had had close, durable ties with Italy, and the emperors cherished the Roman ideal. The German Romanesque churches, however many towers they carry, preserved the antique style. The work of their builders was facilitated by the existence of impressive Roman buildings still standing in many of the imperial centers. Because the Romanesque churches of Germany and Italy conformed to the same models, they resemble one another strongly. Italy did not have to copy or revive Roman building styles: an abundance of ancient edifices served as models, and her artisans, without break or diminished skill, pursued their traditional techniques. But medieval France was different: she lay outside the imperial world and, save in the south, had little continuity with the Roman world. Politically she lacked the kind of stability and unity which the empire imposed on Germany, and culturally she lacked the homogeneity of papal Italy.

The variations in the French Romanesque style are immediately apparent. Their variety is one facet of the regional individuality that marked everything, including the spoken language, and has its roots in history and human geography. French, as it emerged from Latin, developed two main kinds of speech: *la langue d'oc*, spoken by the people whose land fronted on the Mediterranean, and *la langue d'oïl*, the language of the north. The difference in architectural language is analogous. In the northern provinces of Normandy and the Ile de France, Roman buildings were rare. With nothing to emulate, planners and builders had to originate and experiment. The churches they built were the proving ground for daring ventures. Ungainly and untidy, they still vibrate with the excitement of pushing beyond the already known and tried, beyond the antique modes toward the unknown and glorious – toward the style known as Gothic.

The distinctive elements associated with the Gothic style–the pointed arch, the flying buttress, the ribbed vault–had all appeared separately in earlier edifices. By combining them advantageously, the lay architects (who begin to appear early in the thirteenth century) and master masons extended the structural potentials of each element, so that within the limitations imposed by the technological and economic resources of their time each attained its maximum expression. Nothing less than a new aesthetic purpose drove these men. They sought to obtain the greatest interior space at the greatest possible height, a sacred space to be lighted through openings of the greatest possible size. They designed and built the marvelous cathedrals that within an incredibly short time made the Ile de France a prodigy of noble beauty. In these cathedrals we can see how versatile the creators were in gathering the mass of masonry walls and vaults into slender tubular shafts and ribs of expertly dressed stones. A kind of architectural dissection seems to have taken place, in which the extraneous has been eliminated so that the skeletal frame stands naked, straight, and slim, with an outside system of flying buttresses to give it the necessary support. To fill the large wall spaces between the masonry, the builders used glass painting, an art form rarely employed before. The stained-glass windows set in elegant stone traceries transmute the light into a preternatural substance and make the interior atmosphere luminous and almost palpable.

We know the time and place in which the Gothic style materialized, and we know who provided the incentive, the opportunity, and the funds; but we do not know the name of the originator. In 1140 the Abbot Suger of Saint Denis, wishing to modernize the choir of his church, assembled master artisans "from all parts of the kingdom." He needed space for twenty Masses to be said simultaneously; more importantly, perhaps, he longed to provide a setting worthy of the blessed relics of the "Apostle of all Gaul," and the other holy treasures he had accumulated, and to make this church of the royal abbey the peer of Constantinople's Santa Sophia. He himself left an account of the momentous enterprise, but he did not name the artist-engineer who presided over the meeting of talent and experience that produced the Abbey of Saint Denis.

Early and High Gothic coincided with the rise of scholasticism, that structured system of thought so expressive of a society which launched the Crusades and in which wealth and learning, authority and the arts, were all enlisted in the Church's service. And as this philosophy dominated the medieval mind, so the Gothic cathedrals dominated the rising urban landscape. Intellectual and architectural activity alike expressed Western Europe's religious orientation. Both glorified God and proclaimed the beauty of His creations; both channeled their society's extraordinary vigor and daring dreams; both sought to encompass and to systematize sacred dogma and all worldly knowledge. The cosmology of the Middle Ages can be read in Saint Thomas Aquinas's great compendium; it is also evoked by the didactic sculptures that are an integral part of every Gothic cathedral—indeed "an encyclopedia carved in stone."

And yet these Gothic masterpieces were not always cherished or everywhere admired. Giorgio Vasari, the historian and critic, architect of the Uffizi Palace, who named the style, judged it "monstrous and barbarous"; he complained at the prevalence of Gothic churches—"so numerous that they sickened the world"—and explained that such an "abomination of architecture" was the invention of the Goths, "for, after they had ruined the ancient buildings, and killed the architects in the wars, those who were left constructed buildings in this style." Vasari's was the voice and judgment of Italy. There, in the marvelous decades between the work of Brunelleschi (1377–1446) and that of Michelangelo (1475–1564), architecture, along with painting and sculpture, was formed by optical theory, by archaeological study of antique statuary and buildings, by the development of canons of taste, and by the sure hand of genius.

From the thirteenth century on, the flame of the Renaissance had fed on Western Europe's discovery and study of the antique spirit. And when the new art of printing, developed in the second half of the fifteenth century, turned out in its first five decades some eight million books, the range of the antique methods, inquiries, and accomplishments was at hand for all to absorb. Among the recovered treasures was the unique manuscript of a building manual written in the Augustan age. Vitruvius's remarkable *Essay on Architecture*, published in Latin in 1486, detailed the structures and styles, materials and methods used in the constructions of imperial Rome. This comprehensive survey named and described professionally the Greek "orders," the Doric, Ionic, and Corinthian. Vitruvius became the textbook in which generations of architects were rigorously schooled.

Thus, the churches of the Renaissance were designed in the manner of Greek and Roman temples. Aesthetic commitment to the antique mode ended Western Europe's continuous architectural development; the completeness of the break is apparent in the early Renaissance churches, where semicircular Roman arches have ousted the pointed arch, the signature of the Gothic style. Brunelleschi's dome on the Florence cathedral, 1420–1434, was constructed on Gothic principles, formed by separate inner and outer shells. Subsequently the Roman method, making interior and exterior in one piece, lightened the enormous weight; architects could turn their attention to the supporting drum; they pierced it with many windows and surrounded it with columns. Outlined against the sky, the dome rather than the spire became the new symbol of faith.

The artists of the Renaissance who broke with the medieval system were true children of the Church. Yet we know that the introduction of the antique inevitably accelerated other changes in Europe's intellectual climate. Some men reassessed the social and political structure as the growing secular power of monarchs came into conflict with the Papacy's claim to supreme authority, and merchant princes felt constrained by the Church's economic orientation. These men re-examined the foundations of Christian theology, religion, and morality. They called in vain for reforms within the Papacy in the centuries before Martin Luther's Augsburg Confession, in 1530, ushered in the Reformation.

In the twelve hundred years separating Constantine's Edict of Milan and Luther's Augsburg Confession, the Church had enforced her unity and universality, seeking like a watchful mother to carry her children "safely from time into eternity." Yet throughout those centuries dissidents—to the Church they were all heretics—appeared sporadically, indicating that spiritual dissatisfactions were endemic in Europe. One group of heretics sought a desperate salvation outside the Church, in the form of the Christianity adhered to by the Cathars, the "pure." The Cathar religion was a mixture of elements derived from Persian Manichaeist doctrine and early Christian rites. This sect is generally known as the Albigensian, from the city of Albi in southern France, though its center seems to have been Toulouse. To fight this serious rival, whose spiritual leaders were completely dedicated to their version of the Christian life, the Church enforced earlier laws of celibacy for its clergy to match the complete chastity of the *Cathari* or *Perfecti*, as these holy men were called; and to compete with the Cathar deathbed *consolamentum* the Church designed the rite of extreme unction. The Church at the same time waged a crusade of extermination against the Albigenses and subsequently, in 1229, instituted the Office of the Inquisition to ferret out any who might have survived.

A second group of dissidents differed in origin, nature, and eventual development. Among them were the English Lollards, followers of John Wycliffe (1320–1384), and the Hussites, supporters of the Bohemian reformer John Huss, 1369–1415, who carried Wycliffe's teaching into Central Europe. Unlike the Cathar cults, these sects believed in and devoutly accepted the Church's doctrines. But they protested—hence the name Protestant—against the worship of saints, against images and relics, against the laity's second-class position in the spiritual brotherhood, against the monetary basis of compulsory confessions, penances, and indulgences. Their leaders were churchmen and theologians who spoke out for the sacred rights of Christian conscience—so felicitously referred to as "the priesthood of every lay person." To provide the common people with proper spiritual food, the reformers made the Bible available in their common language; Purvey, Wycliffe's secretary, made the first English translation, Luther the first German one, and John Calvin (1509–1564) the first French one. Or, like Huss, the reformers demanded that the Gospel be preached in the language of the congregation and that its members be permitted to receive Holy Communion in both kinds.

Of the early theological reformers, a few, like Wycliffe, died peacefully in their beds—though fifty years later the Church ordered his remains dug up and burned. But most, like Huss, were burned alive. Neither threats of death nor those of eternal damnation could silence the voices of protest. At last these were heard by rulers who valued the support of their Bible-reading subjects and who, for their own political reasons, appreciated the advantages of a state-controlled religious establishment. Foremost among these were the Elector of Saxony and Henry VIII of England. By 1530, Western Christendom was divided between the Roman Catholic Church and the Protestant Churches—the Lutheran, the Anglican, and the Reformed, or Calvinist. The Roman

Catholic Church, through steps taken at the Council of Trent, between 1545 and 1563, cleansed itself of its abuses and, under Ignatius Loyola and his zealous Jesuits, started the Counter Reformation, which effectively stopped the spread of Protestantism. Within the Protestant Churches, the process of dissent and the claims to the right to worship as the individual Christian conscience dictated continued; within the new Protestant faiths other reformers and theologians found in the Bible other roads to salvation.

Europe had enough churches to house the new faiths. With a few alterations and a little rearranging, the existing churches and cathedrals served Protestant congregations—images and shrines were removed, and the pulpit, from which the all-important sermons could be preached, was suitably placed. The first great building of Protestant churches came not because an increase in membership made it necessary, or because men wished to create new architectural forms, but as a result of external circumstances; London's Great Fire of 1666 gave Christopher Wren (1632–1723) the opportunity to design over fifty churches. Wren was not an architect, or even working in the arts; he was an inventor, an astronomer, and one of the founders of the Royal Society. His only apprenticeship was as an observer of the building activity, both secular and religious, commissioned by Louis XIV. In Paris he learned the idiom of "grandeur and elegance" expressed in the colonnaded east front of the Louvre and in the church of Saint Louis des Invalides, the royal chapel, then being constructed. Wren's masterpiece is the mighty Saint Paul's Cathedral, whose dome has been termed one of the most perfect in the world. In his designs Wren achieved a masterly blending of the Classical and the Baroque. What Nikolaus Pevsner calls the "massive forms and the gigantic *excelsior*" of Michelangelo's dome of Saint Peter's had opened the way to the Baroque style. Long before Wren, the infinite possibilities of the Baroque's curved line had been used by churchmen and artists—the Jesuits and pious painters and sculptors—as a way to proclaim the Counter Reformation, to assault the senses with their Catholic message of heavenly jubilation.

The Eastern Orthodox Church is called Eastern because it has maintained a geographic continuity with important Christian centers founded by the Apostles or their immediate followers, at places such as Antioch, Alexandria, Salonika, and Corinth. It calls itself Orthodox because it professes to have preserved to a high degree the doctrine, ritual, and organization of its Apostolic founders. It is sometimes referred to as the Greek Church.

The estrangement between Eastern and Western Christianity began in 330, when Constantinople became the capital of the Eastern Roman Empire. Rome claimed to have retained the supremacy in all matters of Christian faith and morals, a claim instantly rejected by the Patriarchs of Constantinople, Alexandria, Antioch, and Jerusalem. The estrangement deepened when the Empire was divided in 365 and Rome regained her status as the capital of the Western Empire. During the next century Constantinople's Christian strength was enhanced by the misfortunes of her two principal rivals: Alexandria yielded her intellectual primacy when she succumbed to the Monophysite heresy in 451, and Rome her ancient imperial luster when she was sacked by the Goths in 476. East and West drifted further apart when Rome inserted the word *filioque* in the Nicene Creed—thus maintaining that the Holy Ghost proceeds from the Son as well as from God the Father—and Constantinople denied both word and belief. Finally, political and theological differences rent the unity of the Church and led to the Great Schism of 1054.

In the East, from the time of Justinian I (483–565), Church and state were firmly joined: henceforth the emperor ruled both the religious and secular establishments and paid close attention to the preservation of dogma and the spiritual health of the priesthood. The Byzantine emperor retained the aura of divinity accorded the Roman emperors. He was the head of the Church, the viceregent of God, and "the equal of the Apostles." His sanctity is clearly conveyed in the mosaics which cover the interiors of the Eastern churches: like the heads of the Apostles, the emperor's head is circled with a halo. And in the same equation of the royal with the sacred, the angels surrounding Christ the Pantocrator are richly clad in gem-stiffened court robes expressing their adoration in the gestures and genuflections required by court etiquette.

In the East there was no break between early and medieval times. The Byzantine Empire endured more than a thousand years until Constantinople fell in 1453. The last great theological controversy was settled by the end of the ninth century; after that, with creed and doctrine complete, solemn, sensuous rites were designed to bring the Godhead into immediate relationship with the faithful. Holy icons acquired a particular significance. Once the century-long controversy, 726–843, was settled in their favor, painted images were allowed, but statues, still tainted with the charge of paganism, were forbidden. A holy icon, it was thought, partook of the presence and power of that which it delineated: the icon effectively brought the invisible into the visible world. Thus the Orthodox Church devoted itself to preserving and proclaiming its dogma and, as theology's most sacred duty, to initiating the faithful into the mysteries of the liturgy. Resisting any doctrinal changes, the Church's ancient character remained intact—a stability reflected in the stability of her sacred architecture.

When Constantine moved his capital to Byzantium, the Roman world had two basic architectural forms suitable for churches: the rectangular, flat-roofed, aisled basilica and the circular building—usually a mausoleum—roofed with a low dome. The former, so well suited to liturgical needs, did not satisfy the wish to symbolize spatially the power of Christian hope and salvation, the terrible beauty of Christ's Incarnation. The domed roof was attractive—from the outside its swelling curve joined earth and sky, and from the inside the inverted bowl was a celestial cyclorama scaling the heaven's vault to human dimensions. To combine the two—the liturgically correct with the aesthetically desirable—presented an architectural problem: how to place a round dome over a square base.

In the last decades of the fifth century, or the first decades of the sixth, the problem was solved. Whether the structural elements had already existed in Roman construction or whether, as is more generally thought, the Byzantine architects utilized structural inventions discovered in Persia, Armenia, or Syria, they suddenly possessed two valid solutions. One method used squinch arches, that is arches placed diagonally within the internal angles to fill in the right angles until they could support an octagonal superstructure; the other used pendentives, that is, spherical triangles whose apexes, resting on the four supporting columns set in a square, formed curved bases to accommodate the circular dome. Without preliminary experiments, without partial or tentative efforts, the architects of Constantinople seem to have proceeded directly to create two mighty domed basilicas—Saint Irene, built in 532, and that sublime architectural masterpiece the Santa Sophia, erected and decorated by ten thousand workmen in an incredibly short span of six years, 532–537. In the former, windows set into the high drum under the dome added a pleasing dignity to the church and established a precedent which was to become a tradition. Of the latter, whose golden dome seemed to be suspended from heaven, it is recorded that at the consecration ceremonies, when the great Justinian entered his church through the Royal Gates with the Patriarch and slowly proceeded alone up the nave, he stood at the ambo and, having praised God for having permitted him to complete so marvelous a temple, looked around and said softly, proudly, "O Solomon, I have surpassed thee."

If Eastern Orthodoxy was content to retain its theology unchanged, it did not remain confined to its original territory. The creation of new patriarchates showed its northward expansion into the Balkans and Russia, its eastward flow to the lands bordering the Black Sea and southward up the Nile to Ethiopia. Nor were the Byzantine architects content with the mastery they had attained in the early domed churches. They created the cruciform design—the cross-in-a-square—which has been called the architecture of the Incarnation; in later Byzantine times this design was used almost universally, as though the Orthodox Church never tired of reiterating her holy truth. The number of domes on a church also multiplied. Subsidiary domes marked the arms of the cross or crowned side chapels until, as in Russia, as many as thirteen rose from a single cathedral. But, whatever the design, the essential quality of the Orthodox churches, expressed in the unbroken lines of its exterior walls and the compact nature of its interior space, was the unity of the congregation, the fellowship of believers.

It is in their interior decoration—the delicate carving on capitals, the commanding figures wrought in mosaic or painted in prescribed arrangement on walls and ceilings—that the Byzantine churches sing their glorious hosannas. The celestial is quickly related to the earthly. The dome was Heaven, and from its full height Christ the Pantocrator looked down on the nave filled with the faithful, the worshiping Church on earth. The pendentives symbolized the sturdy links between the two—and here the Apostles were placed. The church's interior spoke with sweet strength to those who had ears to hear its divine message.

Houses of God built in the modern idiom are now found everywhere, and in a landscape filled with factories, supermarkets, amusement halls, and the like the surface resemblance of modern churches to secular structures seems to strip them of their sanctity, or make them seem in questionable taste or frankly profane. But contemporary religious structures are also expressions of the continuing development of religion. Modern houses of God are in fact the product of two separate, complex modern movements—in architecture and in liturgy. The modern church is, in effect, the result of a dialogue between architects and theologians.

A modern building is conceived of as the integument surrounding the space required for a specific purpose, whether of working or living. The success or failure of a particular structure is determined first by how well it serves its function, and only secondarily by its aesthetic arrangement. Similarly, the primary purpose of the modern liturgical movement is to express the twentieth century's concepts of faith and religious practice, just as the Gothic style reflected the religious needs and aims and way of life of the society that gave it form.

The modern liturgical movement began early in this century under the impetus of the strongly pastoral Catholic liturgical movement in Belgium; it was strengthened and shaped by German theological and intellectual findings. Certain outstanding Church scholars reviewed Western Europe's long, rich liturgical and architectural developments and, cutting away the accretions of the centuries, revealed the original Church practices —direct in their sacred meaning and always congregational in their form. The purest symbol of Christ in His Church was the Christian altar, and the most venerable tradition was the church as the Eucharistic room. This tradition had been faithfully preserved by the Eastern Orthodox Church, which had never permitted more than a single altar in a church; if another one was needed, a *parakklesion*, a side chapel, in a separate structure, was added.

In the dialogue between architect and theologian, the architect is not asked to design an edifice that "looks like a church," with a built-in religious atmosphere, or one that feels like a church, evoking the Christian mystery by its magnitude, by subtle vistas and a twilight cloud. He is asked to design a building that will function as a house for the Eucharistic assembly, as a place for the liturgy. To create this is enough. "How dreadful is this place! this is none other but the house of God, and this is the gate of heaven": these words, part of the liturgy used in consecrating a church, though spoken in a Christian context, have an ancient and universal sound. They would serve wherever men have fashioned out of their faith a house for their God.

Church of Qalaat Sem an

Viollet

The church of Qalaat Sem an, in Syria, was built between 587 and 590 around the pillar on which Saint Simeon Stylites, the first and most famous of the pillar monks, lived for thirty years. It began as the object of pilgrimages, when fifth-century believers sought out the holy man for advice and instruction. The photograph above shows the apse of the basilica.

146

Sant' Apollinare in Classe in Ravenna commemorated a foreigner who was also both martyr and saint; this noble basilica was erected over his tomb. The tower alongside it was built during the Middle Ages. The interior surfaces depict in gold and vivid colors saints and Apostles, earthly rulers as well as the heavenly host.

Sant' Apollinare in Classe, Ravenna; built 533–536, consecrated 549

On the site of the martyrium built over the saint's body in Ravenna, the Emperor Justinian and his empress, Theodora, erected the elegant basilica of San Vitale. Subtly infused with Eastern elements, San Vitale has a proto-Byzantine quality. The apse *(left)* and additional side apses were used for storing holy vestments and sacramental dishes. The altar, free-standing and bare of ornaments, stood on a platform with two steps.

Interior, San Vitale, Ravenna; begun 522, consecrated 547. *Anderson-Giraudon*

San Ambrogio, Milan

The church of San Ambrogio in Milan, dedicated to Ambrose, a bishop who was later canonized, is an important Romanesque building with Lombard architectural details. Its construction was begun under Ambrose himself, in 386; the next year Saint Augustine was baptized here by the saintly bishop. The church was altered between 789 and 859 to accommodate additions; still later, from 1098 to 1126, it was completed as it now stands, the nave vaulted and domed. The photograph above shows a part of the atrium —the only one in a Lombard church—with one of its two flanking towers.

148

San Lorenzo, Milan   *Brogi-Giraudon*

Santa Maria, Castelseprio

Saint Donat, Zadar   *Photos: Mella*

When the fourth-century church of San Lorenzo in Milan *(above, left)* was rebuilt in the sixteenth century, its original form was preserved. Of the three chapels behind the altar, one still has its fourth-century mosaics.

The fresco cycle painted on the walls of the small Santa Maria at Castelseprio, near Milan *(above, right)*, was discovered when a baroque altar was being removed for safekeeping during World War II. Falling plaster revealed paintings which go back to the ninth century, or even the seventh – authorities differ.

Saint Donat, in Zadar, Yugoslavia *(right)*, with its fortress-like elements, was erected in the ninth century on the foundations of an existing Roman temple, traces of which are still visible. It is now an archaeological museum.

Church in Greenstead, Essex   *Radio Times Hulton Picture Library*

The so-called "Saxon church" in Greenstead, Essex *(above)*, was built of split logs about 1015. Most early British churches utilized bricks from Roman buildings.

Benedictine abbey, Corvey

The Benedictine abbey of Corvey, on the Weser River in Germany, erected from 873 to 885, during Carolingian times, was so named because it was founded by monks from Corbie, in France. Shown at right is the *Westwerk*, as the western side is called in German: the entrance hall, low and vaulted, and a chapel above, opening toward the nave. The quarters for the monks, arranged in orderly fashion around the church, carry out the wise principles laid down by Saint Benedict for communal monastic life ; the location of dormitories, refectories, and storehouses followed the plans he drew up.

Church of Notre Dame, Jumièges   *ND-Giraudon*

Started in 1040, consecrated in 1067, the Church of Notre Dame at Jumièges still speaks
in the language of Norman architecture, that form of the Romanesque style most consistently used in the West. In churches as in castles, the builders created bold and massive forms which, transplanted to England by William the Conqueror, were faithfully
reproduced in Ely, Durham, and other English churches. The two-tower façade, which
appealed to these Norman builders and which the French and English adopted as their
own, seems to have made its first appearance in Strasbourg.

Entrance, Modena Cathedral   *Alinari-Giraudon*

The cathedral of Modena, completed in the thirteenth century, reveals the city's Etruscan beginnings. Adhering to the traditional basilican form, the artisans concentrated on beautiful and delicate ornamentation, as in the entrance shown above, and they created one of the masterpieces of the Italian Romanesque style.

Modena Cathedral, begun 1099

San Miniato al Monte, Florence; 1013   *Alinari-Giraudon*

The name Tuscany is derived from Etruscan, and the Tuscans preserved the grace and refinement of the Etruscan spirit while absorbing the assurance and simplicity of the Roman conquerors. The Florentine church of San Miniato al Monte anticipates in its classical proportions the elegance of the Renaissance, as its use of black and white marble was to be followed with striking results in later and larger churches. Bright colors decorate the open-timber roof *(above)*; translucent marble makes the interior luminous.

153

The German way of breaking the monotony of the early Christian basilica was very different from the French. In Saint Michael's at Hildesheim, the earliest example extant of a German Romanesque exterior, two chancels, with towers over both crossings, were employed, with staircase turrets on the ends of both transepts. Saint Bernward, the bishop who created the plan of Saint Michael's, was, to quote Pevsner, a man "foremost in writing, experienced in painting, excellent in the science and art of bronze founding and in all architectural work."

At Worms *(left)* the same dual plan was followed. Because the cathedral is apsidal at both ends, the entrances, located behind the twin circular towers enclosing stairways, opened directly into the aisles.

Worms Cathedral, 1175–1181

Mella

La Madeleine, Vézelay; erected 1089–1206, restored by Viollet-le-Duc, mid-nineteenth century

Tympanum, La Madeleine, Vézelay   *Giraudon*

One of the most perfect of the French Romanesque churches, La Madeleine at Vézelay, from which Saint Bernard preached the Second Crusade, is also one of the most famous. In its superbly carved tympanum *(above)* and in the rich variety of its capitals, seen in the interior opposite, we witness the return of the plastic sense, which for the first time since antiquity appeared in the religious architecture of the eleventh century. By the close of the twelfth century, at Vézelay and at Moissac *(overleaf)*, sculpture had been created whose aesthetic quality was commensurate with that of the churches themselves.

155

Mosaic, Cathedral of Monreale, Palermo   *Alinari*

Vézelay's most sacred treasure, the relics of the saint whose name the church bears, made it a favored object of pilgrimages. The road of the pilgrims led from Vézelay, by way of Le Puy, Conques (or Périgueux), and Moissac to Spain. Or, from Chartres, pilgrims traveled by way of Orléans, Tours, Poitiers, Les Saintes Maries to Santiago de Compostela in Spain.

While Western Europe was creating new masterpieces, as at Vézelay and Moissac, the Norman rulers of Sicily retained the form of the early Christian basilica and utilized the Byzantine idiom long resident in the island. The cloisters of the Cathedral of Monreale at Palermo, all that remain of a Benedictine monastery dating from 1174, are the finest of their kind. Their solemn elegance hardly prepares the eye for the drama inside the church, where the walls are covered with mosaics of gold and rich colors. Saints and angels appear close at hand and Biblical scenes, as in the detail above, teach and delight. Precise arcaded line and vivid scene lead to a magnificent Christ framed in the apse.

157

Opposite: Bell tower and dome, Siena Cathedral, 1245–1380. *Anderson-Giraudon*

The civic pride, the energy, and the talents of the Sienese went into the building and adornment of their stupendous and strikingly beautiful cathedral. The bravura of the zebra-like striping on piers, walls, and squinches, the marble floor richly incised by the city's master pavement designers, the sprawling structure itself *(opposite)*, astride a stepped platform: every aspect of extraordinary form and decoration make this one of the finest of the Italian churches.

Detail of pavement, Siena   *Anderson-Giraudon*

Interior, Siena

159

Church of San Francesco, Assisi   *Fritz Henle*

Assisi clusters on a spur of Mount Subasio; here Saint Francis was born in 1182; on the
bare earth of the plain where the hill begins he died in 1226. The saint and the hill define
the nature of the immense structures that crown the spur. Built, between 1228 and 1253,
on massive masonry foundations and following the rise of the land are two superimposed
churches, an upper and a lower. The shrines were visited by vast numbers of pilgrims
whom the saint's life and message of love and brotherhood–did Saint Francis not sing
to Brother Sun and Sister Earth and Brother Wind?–filled with the presence of God.

In the aisleless interiors, solemn, dim, mysterious, Cimabue and Giotto lovingly
pictured the story of the saint. The location of the monastery and churches of San
Francesco in the heart of the town reminds us that the Franciscans, like the Dominicans,
did not seek solitude but settled in busy communities; they desired churches capable of
holding crowds of people gathered to hear them preach.

Church of the Vera Cruz, Segovia

Mella

Les Saintes-Maries-de-la-Mer *ND-Giraudon*

A modest miniature copy of Jerusalem's Church of the Holy Sepulcher, the Church of the Vera Cruz in Segovia *(above)*, stands under the guard of the ancient fortress, the Alcázar. Built in the early thirteenth century, the church was at one time owned by the Templars, the order founded to defend the holy places of Palestine and protect pilgrims from attack.

The fortified church of Les Saintes-Maries-de-la-Mer *(right)*, on the Mediterranean coast of France, is a notable landmark. Built in the twelfth century, it reflects the unsettled times in which it was erected. The Mithraic chapel which once occupied the site is now the crypt; Saint Sara, patron of gypsies, is honored there, and every May gypsies from all over Europe flock to honor her.

161

Saint Michel d'Aiguille, Puy-de-Dome.
Burton Holmes / Ewing Galloway

Saint Michel d'Aiguille *(left)*, one of the Cluniac pilgrimage churches, was built in the twelfth century in the Puy-de-Dome district of the Auvergne. Formed by volcanic activity, the area's rocks are of tufa and colored pumice, and its churches have utilized their special characteristics. Lava of different colors patterns their walls, and the stone-vaulted roofs are made of blocks of pumice, feather-light.

Crypt, Saint Denis

In the Romanesque crypt of the royal abbey of Saint Denis *(right)* are the tombs of the kings and queens of France, from the Capetian Louis VII, the Abbot Suger's king, to the Bourbon Louis XVI and his queen, Marie Antoinette. Of the glorious church the Abbot built (1132–1144), little remains, and that little is mostly rebuilt and restored. Wars and revolution have wrecked the monument whose creation marks the beginning of the Gothic style.

Sens Cathedral

The cathedral at Sens, erected in 1143, very soon after Saint Denis, shows us what Suger's building looked like. The arches of arcade, gallery, and clerestory – for the earliest Gothic elevation had three stories – were pointed and gave a triumphant height to the nave, shown above. More and more emphasis was to be upon verticality. As the columned interior of the Romanesque style set up a motion that carried the worshiper irresistibly toward the altar, so the Gothic style, mounting higher and ever higher, lifted the eye toward heaven.

163

La Merveille, Mont-Saint-Michel

ND-Giraudon

Mont-Saint-Michel, off the Atlantic coast of France, is one of the great fortified monasteries, containing within its walls buildings devoted to secular as well as religious activities. The cloister, La Merveille *(left)*, shows the pointed arch which delighted the builders of the thirteenth century. The monastery was restored by Viollet-le-Duc in the mid-nineteenth century.

Mont-Saint-Michel

The wide west façade of Notre Dame at Paris has a central rose window 42 feet in diameter, flanked by high windows over which rise the two western towers. One of the finest creations of the Gothic builders, characteristically French, it was the model for many of the cathedrals that were soon to be built. Symmetry and balance were achieved by the ground plan, which placed the transept almost halfway between the towered west end and the elaborate double ambulatory around the apse. The cruciform design—the long east-west axis cut by the shorter north-south transept which the early Christian basilica adopted from the tombs of the period of Constantine—is here merely suggested: the ends of the transept hardly project beyond the outer aisles.

Interior, Notre Dame
Paris; 1163–1235.
Giraudon

The western towers of Notre Dame from the Seine   *Fritz Henle*

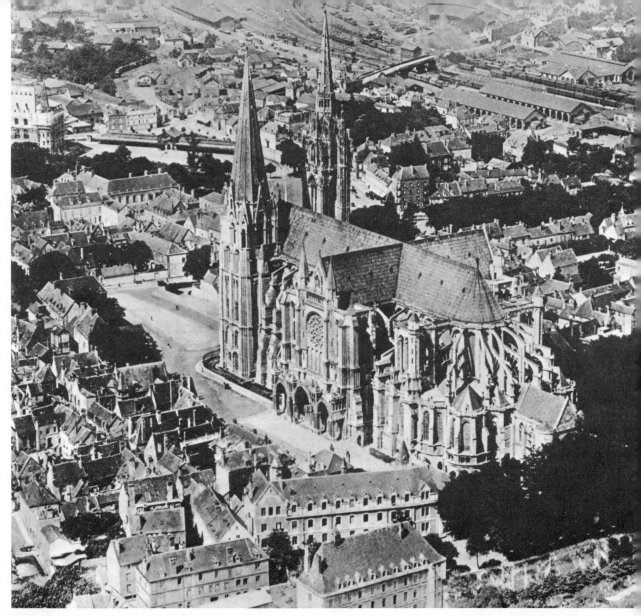

Opposite and above: Chartres Cathedral   *Aero-Photo, Paris*

When Chartres was rebuilt in 1194, after a fire, the changes made—a new type of pier, a more intense verticality in the elevation, and a vastly simplified vaulting—ushered in the High Gothic style. Chartres has a bewilderment of riches. The Gothic invention, tracery—the ornamental stone pattern-work of the windows—became more delicate and daring; in the hundred and thirty superb windows which lighten the walls, tracery and glass create a duet of form and color. The towers flanking the western façade have spires; the south one, simpler, was built in 1145; the north one, constructed in 1506, is considered one of the most beautiful in Europe.

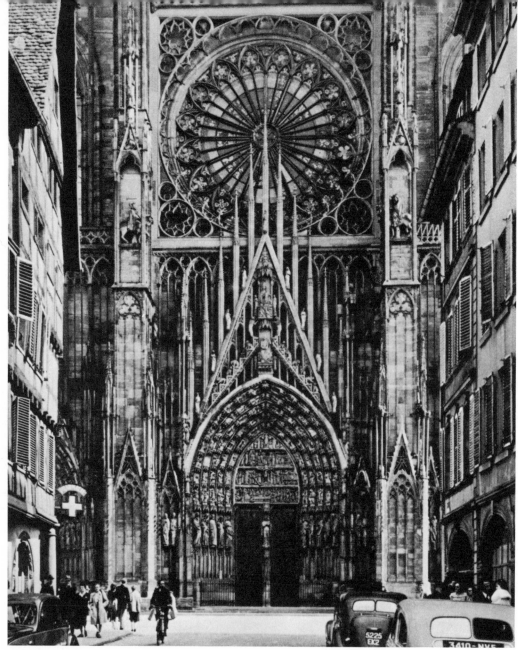

Strasbourg Cathedral   *Hürlimann*

The cathedrals grew and changed over the centuries. Strasbourg *(above)*, one of the masterpieces of French devotional art, in its plan of 1015 sounded a new and important note when its western facade was given two towers, a motif adopted by Norman church builders at Jumièges and in England. The Romanesque choir erected in 1179 had a Gothic-style nave added in 1318; in 1439 the spire rose to give it its present mighty form.

The thirteenth-century cathedral at Colmar shows the traditional plan, the basic theme on which the genius of many people was to create an endless series of masterly and beautiful variations: the eastern apsidal end, the transept, and, at the western end, the tower-flanked portal. The aerial view below shows how such cathedrals nested in the busy heart of the cities they graced.

Colmar Cathedral

The Sainte Chapelle, in Paris, was the royal chapel built from 1243 to 1248 by Saint Louis for the devotional needs of the kings of France. The lofty upper chapel *(below)* is sheathed in glass, each window 15 feet wide and 50 feet high. The beautifully carved dado, repeating the arched outline of the windows, discreetly provided the royal worshipers with privacy.

La Sainte Chapelle, Paris

Sainte Cécile at Albi

Photos: Giraudon

The fortress church of Sainte Cécile, at Albi *(left)*, close to the Spanish border, was influenced by the Catalan style. Built from 1277 to 1392, it is a stark massive form, shorn of buttresses and flying buttresses, declaring its militant defiance. It was a friars' church, and its nave, long, vaulted, and decorated, the widest in France —59 feet—was capable of holding the large numbers of people who came to hear the friars preach.

The church of Saint Urbain at Troyes, with the same slim, brittle elegance as the Sainte Chapelle, is an edifice of major size. It was built at the end of that extraordinary, magnificent, unflagging outpouring of masterpieces which Saint Denis ushered in. In the first half of the thirteenth century, about a hundred and fifty cathedrals, each one touched with originality, were built in France. The later churches lacked daring and creativity; no longer exploring the possibilities of the Gothic style, they accepted what had been done, and added to the number of examples without enriching the architectural language.

Gargoyle, Saint Urbain, Troyes; 1262–1277

Salisbury Cathedral

In its ample setting of green-sward and mighty elm trees, Salisbury cathedral *(left)*, begun in 1220, has an air of majestic repose. Its 400-foot spire is the tallest in England.

Durham Cathedral

ENGLISH GOTHIC CATHEDRALS. The impulse which began at Saint Denis and flowered in northern France was carried to England by her Norman conquerors. There, Norman faith and energy created its own Gothic style and constructed its own masterpieces. Jumièges *(see page 151)* is the noble parent of Ely, Durham, and Winchester. In England the terms Early English, Decorated, and Perpendicular correspond to High and Late Gothic on the continent. The English possessed a rich stream of inventiveness which makes each cathedral a monument of splendor.

Superbly situated on the crest of a hill, Durham *(right)* is one of England's greatest cathedrals, not only for its fine Norman nave, but also because here the master builders first constructed ribbed vaults, essential to the Gothic style; this technique was subsequently used and developed on the continent. Between 1242 and 1290, the eastern transept, the "Chapel of the Nine Altars," was added, with the dignified central tower. Despite the long period of time over which it was built, 1099–1133, the cathedral has an organic unity.

174

Ely *(right)* is famous for its fine Norman nave with timbered roof and especially for its octagon-shaped towered crossing, designed by Alan Walsingham in 1322.

The core of Winchester cathedral *(below)* –nave and chancel, transept and tower– is Norman, dating from 1079 to 1093. From 1371 to 1440, under the guidance of William of Wykeham and his successors, this core was covered by a veneer of Perpendicular. Of all the mighty medieval cathedrals built in Europe, Winchester is the longest, measuring 560 feet.

Ely Cathedral

Winchester Cathedral

Photos: Radio Times Hulton Picture Library

Wells Cathedral

Radio Times Hulton Picture Library

The above view of the cathedral at Wells, built from 1186 to about 1425, is from the garden of the bishop's palace. Serene, relaxed, noble – it has all the qualities of the English Gothic sanctuaries.

English cathedrals, whether they grew and were transformed from Norman beginnings or were started late and maintained a uniform style, achieved a special and distinctive national articulation. When, in 1534, Henry VIII became "Protector and only Supreme Head of the Church and Clergy of England," these cathedrals proved entirely suitable for the new liturgy of their congregations.

The small cathedral of Saint Peter's in Geneva *(right)* is a neat example of the modest beginning of changing styles and tastes in the early thirteenth century. A graceful spire was raised above its pitched roof and tower, and then a portico was added, as if, in Pevsner's apt words, "it was deemed necessary to furnish a rational and classical approach to the Christian mysteries." Next to it is an older church, not as fashionable but still filled with the echo of the lectures Calvin delivered there and the passionate sermons John Knox preached when, from 1554 to 1559, he served the English community as pastor.

Saint Peter's, Geneva

Cathedral at Tournai

The fine black marble of the cathedral of Tournai *(left)* in Belgium, built between 1066 and 1338, unifies three distinct styles in parts constructed at three widely separated times. The cathedral began as a simple Romanesque nave. Eighty years later, in 1146, the addition of the circular-ended transept, the four towers, and the central lantern tells us of the town's growth and pride. Two hundred years afterward, a High Gothic chevet in the fine French manner brought a new element to the huge structure.

177

Cathedral at Minden

The early Westphalian Gothic style was slow to give up the rounded arch of the Romanesque style. Minden *(above)*, has the distinctive design of the *Hallenkirche*, "hall churches," where, because the nave and aisles are of almost equal height, there was no need for triforium and clerestory.

178

Erfurt cathedral *(left)*, also a German hall church, has extremely high traceried windows. The roof, in one immense span, covers the nave and lofty aisles. At the top of the stairs is a porched doorway, elaborately carved – a response to the French influence.

The lofty spire of the cathedral at Ulm *(below)*, built from 1377 to 1477, is its greatest distinction. Spires of extraordinary height – this one shoots up 630 feet – distinguish the Late Gothic style from the High Gothic in which the several towers were grouped.

Erfurt Cathedral   *Viollet*

Cathedral at Ulm

Opposite: Interior, Saint Laurence, Nürnberg

The 446-foot spire of Saint Stephen's *(right)* dominates Vienna. The present church was built after a disastrous fire in 1285 had destroyed a twelfth-century Romanesque church. The spire, almost a hundred years in the building, was completed in 1433. The Gothic-type tiles on the roof were destroyed in World War II.

Saint Stephen's, Vienna

Saint Vitus, Prague   *Foto Marburg*

The basic floor plan of Saint Vitus in Prague *(right)*, one of Central Europe's most famous cathedrals, is French, though its decorative details are phrased in the local idiom. Nave and chancel are structurally divided, and the apsidal end has a true chevet. In following the French Gothic design, Prague aligned herself with the powerful monastic voices that fought heresy–Saint Vitus himself stood firm against the Hussite threat.

The interior of Saint Laurence *(Lorenzkirche)* at Nürnberg *(opposite)*, built from 1445 to 1472, is in the late "Romantic" style of hall church, with wide, windowed arcades and wide, lofty aisles.

Monastery of San Jeronimo, Belem, Lisbon; 1499. *Viollet*

Old and New Cathedrals, Salamanca

On the bank of the Tormes River in Spain lies Salamanca *(above)*, the town clustering close to the Old and New Cathedrals. The Old Cathedral, a fine thirteenth-century Romanesque building, was not altered when the Gothic style swept over Europe. Instead, next to it, the Spaniards built the New Cathedral, begun in the sixteenth century and finished in the eighteenth, which incorporates the Gothic, the Plateresque—the ornate decoration favored by silversmiths and applied to stone and wood—and the Baroque styles.

Cathedral at Burgos

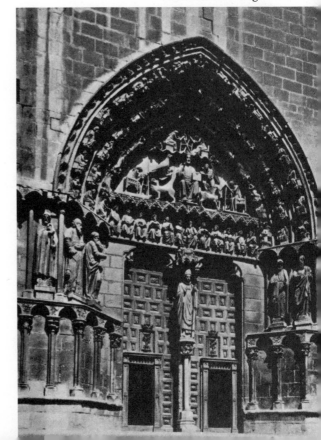

Burgos Cathedral, where the heroic Cid is buried, began as a handsome basilican church in 1220; its present splendor dates from 1567 and shows the influence of master builders who came to Spain from Cologne and Nürnberg when the rulers of Burgos had political ties with the German princes. As in a German hall church, the aisles are wide and lofty, but lower than the nave, a reminder of the basilican design; as in other Spanish churches, there are chapels set within the buttresses, and the sculpture is rich in Iberian themes. The beautiful doorway to the south transept *(right)*, created around 1250, is wholly Spanish in iconography.

The cloister of the monastery of San Jeronimo in Belem, a suburb of Lisbon *(opposite)*, with its lion fountain and delicate sculpture, has a two-storied arcade with the arches richly carved in the Late Gothic style. The design and ornamentation, with its faint Moorish accent, hint at the opulence Portugal enjoyed when wealth from African and Asian discoveries made her the envy of Europe.

Opposite: Orvieto Cathedral

Milan, after Seville, possesses the largest medieval cathedral in Europe. As many as fifty architects from German cities worked on the cathedral *(below)*, built between 1385 and 1485, and a Frenchman designed and executed its three immense traceried windows, the largest in the world. What is wholly Italian is the exuberance of its sculptured stone: its wonderful frets, the ornamentation used at the intersection of right angles, its 135 pinnacles, and its more than 2200 statues.

The plan of the cathedral at Orvieto is basilican; but how do we classify the black and white striped interior with its lofty cylindrical columns, its timbered roof and pointed windows? All this is secondary, however, to its extraordinary, glowing Gothic façade *(opposite)*, with its gables and traceried rose window, its mosaics and exquisite sculpture.

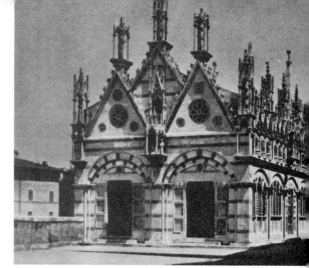

Santa Maria della Spina, Pisa

Pisa, renowned for her magnificent Romanesque cathedral, also created, in 1323, this tiny gem of Gothic architecture, Santa Maria della Spina *(above).*

Milan Cathedral   *Photos: Hürlimann*

Saint Mark's is the supreme glory of Byzantine architecture and art in the
West. Ruskin described it as "a vast illuminated missal, bound with alabaster instead of parchment, studded with porphyry pillars instead of jewels,
and written within and without in letters of enamel and gold." The large, handsome square on which it faces serves as a vast atrium to the cathedral.
Named for the sea city's patron saint, it began as a basilican church erected
in 864 to enshrine Saint Mark's body; it was rebuilt between 1042 and 1085
after the old church had been badly damaged by fire. For the new structure
the Venetians took as their model the Church of the Holy Apostles erected by
Justinian as his mausoleum, which is said to have rivaled the glorious Santa
Sophia. The changes transformed the basilica to the Byzantine plan of a
Greek cross surmounted by domes. More than the model came from Byzantium: many of Saint Mark's greatest treasures were part of the loot brought
back from the sack of Constantinople. To make its interior lovelier and richer
than any other shrine, Venetian trading captains were ordered to bring
home treasures as votive offerings for the city's success in commerce and
war. The bronze horses above the center doorway once were on Nero's
triumphal arch; Constantinople and Alexandria unwillingly contributed
pillars of porphyry, alabaster, and rare colored marbles. To house these
treasures acquired by trade and tribute the Venetians created golden mosaics
covering the interior and framing scenes from the story of the Creation, the
Fall of Man, the miracles of Christ, and the Redemption.

Sometime during the thirteenth century, a crown of gilded timbers was
built up over the domes, and in the fifteenth century the Gothic-type facade,
a delicate stone lacework, made the exterior as opulent as the golden interior.

On its island, the stately white marble church of Santa Maria della Salute, built from 1560 to 1575, rises out of the waters of the Grand Canal in Venice. The pedimented façade, designed in strict accordance with the classical orders, makes a majestic approach to the basilica with its apsidal transepts.

Santa Maria della Salute, Venice — *Fritz Henle*

Pazzi Chapel, Santa Croce, Florence

Basilica, Santo Spirito, Florence *Adelmann*

The Pazzi Chapel *(above)*, within the quiet cloister of the large, beautiful Franciscan church of Santa Croce, in Florence, built from 1294 to 1442, is the first Renaissance church. The genius of Brunelleschi, who planned and built the chapel, in 1420, gave spatial expression to the Renaissance spirit, and the greatest talents of Florence contributed to its quiet perfection. Its façade has elegant architecturally designed medallions by Donatello, and terra-cotta decorations by della Robbia.

The basilica of Santo Spirito *(right)*, also designed by Brunelleschi, was built from 1436 to 1482. The form goes back through the Middle Ages to antiquity, but its effect of "serene order" is the result of the mathematically determined relations of its component parts; for example, Brunelleschi made the height of the nave twice its width, and the ground floor and clerestory of the same height.

Santa Maria del Fiore, Florence

When the city council of Florence decided to erect a cathedral worthy of their prosperous city, they utilized, as its core, the old church of San Reparata. Beginning in 1296, the finest talents were enlisted – Arnolfo di Cambio, Giotto, Andrea Pisano, and Francesco Talenti, in succession – in the task of building the Santa Maria del Fiore. Finally, in 1421, Brunelleschi won the competition for the dome, shown above. Only in 1462 was the dome finished with the lantern *(left)* he had designed for it.

Tet Borsig

The cathedral of Badia, in Fiesole, whose interior
is that of an eleventh-century Romanesque church,
was rebuilt between 1559 and 1566.

Tet Borsig

Saint Peter's, Vatican City, Rome. *Detail from a Piranesi print*

Julius II is remembered as one of the greatest builders the Papacy has known: he was the architect of the Papal States and it was he who in 1506 commissioned Bramante to give Saint Peter's, the holiest church in Western Europe, spatial importance. Through politics and architecture this Pope gave concrete expression to his vision of the Church's dominant position.

When Bramante began the task Saint Peter's was essentially the church Constantine had had erected—a long basilica where the faithful could gather and celebrate the Eucharistic feast. Bramante, however, continuing the Renaissance exploration of space—in studies initiated by Brunelleschi, and carried forward by the finest Italian artists, such as da Vinci—favored a strictly central plan. His design, a model of symmetry, was a Greek cross with four equal apses crowned with a classical dome. Julius II's "amazing decision" to adopt "this symbol of worldliness for his own church," is seen by Pevsner as proof that "the spirit of Humanism had indeed penetrated into the innermost fortress of Christian resistance." Bramante's plan had no clear architectural statement of where the high altar was to be placed.

By 1546, during the papacy of Paul III, when Michelangelo was called on to redesign Saint Peter's, the Church's unity had been shattered by the Reformation. In his glorious additions—the back of Saint Peter's and its stupendous dome—Michelangelo denied the spirit of the Renaissance and subordinated antiquity to Christianity. Before Saint Peter's was consecrated in 1626, another change—an elongation of the nave in the front—restored the longitudinal shape of the basilica. Bernini's masterly colonnade encloses the elliptically shaped approach.

Opposite: The high altar, Saint Peter's.
Ernst Haas/Magnum

Vatican City, Rome.
Ernst Haas / Magnum

195

Santiago de Compostela, Spain

Mella

After Jerusalem and Rome, Santiago de Compostela on the Galician coast of Spain was the greatest object of pilgrimage in Europe. Here the lost tomb of the Apostle James was found miraculously in 813; it was lost again in 1598 when Sir Francis Drake sacked nearby La Coruña and the body was sent for safekeeping to another town. Yet Compostela remained a holy site for the faithful. The cathedral *(left)*, built from the eleventh to the eighteenth century, was constantly enlarged and beautified; it became one of Spain's most magnificent Baroque cathedrals, preserving reminders of its early Romanesque design, its response to French Gothic influences, and Spanish Renaissance elements.

Fulda Cathedral and Saint Michael's

Baroque church at Melk

Melk *(left)*, in Austria, rearing up from the steep rocks above the Danube, was built from 1702 to 1736, at a time when south Germany and Austria were afflicted with a mania for Baroque buildings of colossal size. The church is flanked by vast monastery buildings, the entire monumental structure expressing both the Church militant and the refined sensibility of the eighteenth century.

Church of Fourteen Saints, Bavaria

Baroque and Rococo are different moods of the same style of architecture—a lively and playful style, with a vivacious and fragile sensuousness. If the German church of Vierzehnheiligen (Fourteen Saints) *(right)*, built from 1743 to 1772, were merely a masterpiece of the confectioner's art, our appetite would long since have been satisfied. But the church's interior is a lovely counterpoint of ovals and circles as disciplined as a fugue.

The fine Baroque cathedral at Fulda *(left)* contrasts with the severity of its neighbor, Saint Michael's, one of the old churches of Germany (820–822), seen in the distance.

Saint Paul's, London

To describe Saint Paul's of London *(above)*, built from 1675 to 1710, one must quote Pevsner: "As for the façade of St. Paul's, begun in 1685, it is, with... the two fantastic towers on the sides (designed after 1700), a decidedly Baroque composition. The side elevations are dramatic, though of a secular, palace-like effect.... Inside there is a poignant contrast between the firmness of every part and the spatial dynamics of the whole. The dome is as wide as nave and aisles together – a motif which Wren may have remembered from Ely or from the engravings of such Italian buildings as the Cathedral of Pavia. It adds splendor and surprise to the whole composition."

The Baroque interior of the Bavarian Church-in-the-Meadow *(opposite,* built from 1746 to 1754) at Steingaden, provides a marvelous illusion of limitless space.

Opposite: Interior, Church-in-the-Meadow, Steingaden.   *Fritz Henle*   199

Christianity in the New World

Wren's influence can be seen in the churches that were built in England and in England's overseas colonies. They take their name not from an architect or a style but from a social period—Georgian. Wren's prodigious inventiveness as it expressed itself in the fifty-three churches he designed furnished elements which in endless combinations grace our American cities and landscape. Whatever the details of façade and spire, they all provided the central space and surrounding galleries suited to the preaching requirements of the Protestant faiths.

Saint-Martin's-in-the-Field, London; 1722

Saint Joseph's Cathedral, Bardstown, Kentucky

Even the Roman Catholic Saint Joseph's Cathedral *(above)*, at Bardstown, one of Kentucky's oldest churches, adopted the Georgian idiom, adding only its side chapels and holy images.

Opposite: Georgian church at Litchfield, Connecticut. *André de Dienes*

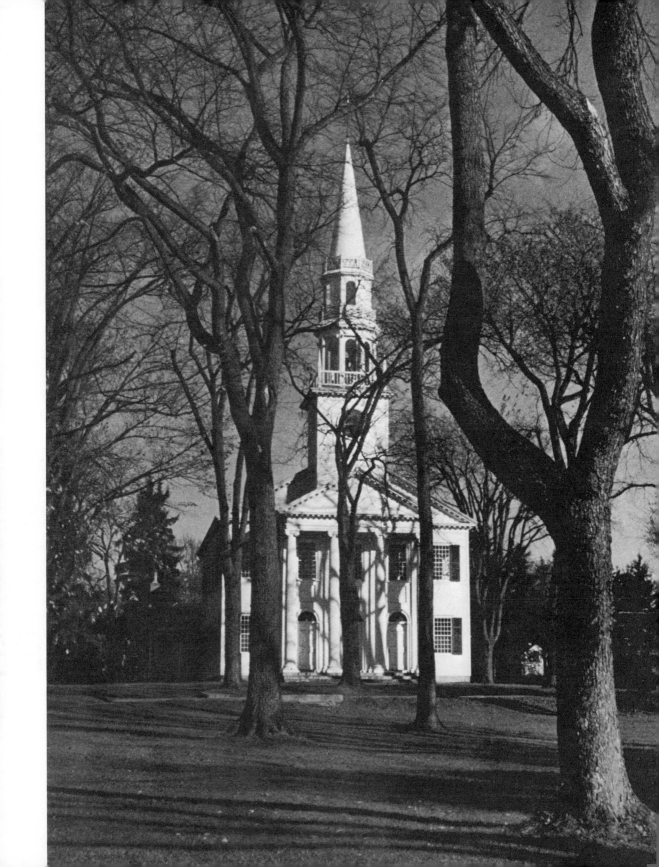

Saint John's Church, Richmond, Virginia, where Patrick Henry
made his great speech of March 1775.

Opposite: Church at Wiscasset, Maine
Photos: Elisofon

Italian mountain church.

Tyrolean mountain chapel. *Walden*

Country Churches

Everywhere in the New World, as well as in Europe, churches grace the countryside. Usually they are small, sturdy, and modest; sometimes they are isolated. There is a timeless quality about them.

These churches serve rural communities: locally built and locally decorated, their styles are dictated by local taste. Like the families which foregather there on the Sabbath and on Holy Days, the buildings shown on the following pages seem to wear their countryside best.

Wayside shrine, Austria. *Dr. Benesch*

204

Saint Duh, Bohinj, Yugoslavia. *Mella*   Are church, Jämtland, Sweden   *S. Larson*

Church at Alberobello, Italy, of *trulli* construction: stone laid without mortar; the conical roofs are also of stone. *Giraudon*

Circular Hagby church, Sweden. *S. Larson*

Hessino church, Sweden; twelfth century

A church near Bern, Switzerland   *Courtesy: Standard Oil Co., N.J.*

Quaker Meeting House, Princeton, New Jersey, finished in 1760; it housed the wounded of both armies – Washington's and Cornwallis' – during the Revolution. *John Borden*

Churches at Volders, Austria (*below*),
and Burgenland, Austria (*right*)

Iona Cathedral in Scotland
Left: Saint Donlough's church near Dublin, Ireland
Opposite: Stave church, Borgund, Norway. *Kostich*

Mission, Taos, New Mexico.   *Andreas Feininger, courtesy* Life

Spanish Churches in the New World

More than a century before the first Pilgrim landed in Massachusetts, the Spaniards had planted in New Spain cultured communities with churches and monasteries. And as Spain spread north and south along the Pacific coast churches and chapels and missions were often the only visible sign of her tenancy. Many of these first religious edifices have deteriorated, many have been replaced with newer structures, and many are revered as landmarks of that first European period.

La Compania, Cuzco, Peru *Frank Scherschel*

Church of Puerto Coeli (Gate of Heaven), Puerto Rico

211

Martin Chambi

The choir of the colonial Cuzco Cathedral in Peru had the opulence, the ornate style of Spanish art found in silver work and tooled leather and in the great cathedrals which crowned the cities of the mother country.

Cliff chapels, Ürgüp, Turkey

Ancient Monasteries

The valley of Goreme, in Turkey, is isolated, desiccated, inhuman; to it came hermits and monks, from the ninth to the eleventh centuries. They carved hundreds of chapels out of the cliffs, chapels which, like that at Ürgüp *(above)*, remain as they were when men painted their walls with the figures of their faith—austere figures from the Old Testament, intense saints already legendary, and always the sad, brooding face of Christ.

Like Saint Simeon, who withdrew from the world to live atop his pillar, small monasteries such as that of Meteora in Greece *(below)*, stood on virtually inaccessible pinnacles—many have a basket contraption that serves as an elevator—offering refuge to monastic communities.

Monastery of Meteora, Greece   *Photos: Mella*

Monastery of Saint Denys, Mount Athos, Greece   *Ewing Galloway*

For a thousand years, continuing the medieval discipline, undisturbed in their fidelity
to tradition, monastic communities have existed on Mount Athos in the mountainous
Greek peninsula of Acte. In such a monastery as is shown above, scholars found, about
seventy-five years ago, a unique manuscript written by a monk, Dionysius. It was a
manual for artists engaged in decorating the interiors of Eastern Orthodox churches,
and furnished a precise iconographic scheme to be followed in the symbolic presentation
of the Church's dogma.

Churches of the East

Santa Sophia (its Greek name is Hagia Sophia–"Holy Wisdom") in Istanbul, has commanded the awe of all who have seen it. Procopius, a historian writing at the time it was built, spoke of "its golden dome, which seems to rest not on solid masonry but is as if suspended from heaven to cover the space." In 1453, the last year it was to serve as a Christian church, it was described by a contemporary as "the heaven upon earth, the throne of the glory of God, the second firmament and chariot of cherubim, the handiwork of God, a marvelous and worthy work."

The genius who planned and directed the architectural magic of Santa Sophia was Anthemius of Tralles, near Ephesus. Assisted by Isidore of Miletus, he succeeded in combining the longitudinal basilica with a dome 107 feet in diameter. What we see today differs, however, from what they created from 532 to 537. Twenty-one years after it was consecrated, the first of many earthquakes damaged the church; Justinian ordered the structure repaired and replaced the dome with a higher one which was strengthened by external buttresses. A severe quake in 989 caused the west arch and the dome to collapse. In 1204 the church was vandalized by the Crusaders and looted of its magnificent objects of silver and gold and precious jewels. Still it survived. More ungainly buttresses were added after later earthquakes. In 1453 the Moslem conquerors turned the building into a mosque and added the four minarets shown below.

The drawing of the interior *(opposite)* made by the Swiss architect Fossati, who was called in to make repairs in 1852, shows Santa Sophia when it served Islam as a mosque. Today, as a museum, it belongs to all faiths.

Opposite and below: Santa Sophia, Istanbul   *Mella*

Whereas Santa Sophia fills a parallelogram 320 feet by 220 feet, the smallest cathedral in the world *(left)*, built about 1250 in Athens, measures but 38 feet by 25 feet; its dome, rising high on an octagonal drum, is 9 feet in diameter. Its religious names have a sonorous sound: Church of the Virgin Gorgoepikoos, or Church of Saint Eleutherios.

Some of the ninety sculptured slabs and fragments embedded in its walls, pleasing items taken from older pagan buildings, are visible in the photograph. The cathedral's modest dimensions, its compact form, so characteristic of many Greek churches, suggest the small sanctuaries within the glorious façade of the temples on the Acropolis.

Ohrid, in Yugoslavia, had a special place in ecclesiastical geography: it was the main stopover on the busy road connecting Rome and Constantinople. Two of its churches reflect the rival cultural traditions which marked eastern Europe from the tenth century to the fourteenth–its Byzantine cathedral and the church of Saint Clement *(left)*. The latter, built about 1300, crouches on a sunny hill overlooking the town but has the dark mysterious interior of other south Serbian churches. Recently it has been cleansed of centuries of soot, coats of varnish, and nineteenth-century decorations, to reveal frescoes painted by an unknown master.

Near the thirteenth-century monastery of Gračanica *(left)*, the battle of Kosovo was fought, the battle which ended Serbian independence and brought in the Turks as conquerors and rulers. Here, the night before the fateful battle, the last Christian king slept before riding out to the "Field of the Blackbirds" to perish with his army. Thousands of pilgrims gather here yearly on Saint Vitus's Day to commemorate the anniversary of that dreadful slaughter. Gračanica is hauntingly beautiful in form–its dome, in the northern Byzantine style, soaring above the clustering elements of the church–and equally rich in its celebrated frescoes.

Russian Churches

Toward the close of the tenth century Byzantine architecture came to Russia. When Prince Vladimir of Kiev established Christianity as the state religion, Kiev attracted architects as well as missionaries. "Mother of the Cities of Russia," Kiev, at the height of its glory, compared its four hundred churches with those of Constantinople. Its cathedral, the Saint Sophia, rebuilt after the Tartar invasion in 1037, set the pattern for ecclesiastical buildings. Just as its design was derived from Constantinople, the mosaics lining its walls had the hieratic and rigid style then favored in Greece. The cruciform, or crossed-domed, basilica remained the basic style, unchanged when Kiev was superseded by Novgorod, and when Novgorod in turn yielded to the primacy of Moscow, early in the fourteenth century.

As the center of political power moved northward the external structure was altered to suit the climate: without deviating from the cross-in-square outline, changes in the shape and disposition of the roof were made imperative by the heavy snows and equally heavy rains. In the north the roof, instead of undulating as it followed the curves of the vaults it sheathed, had four slopes to prevent the accumulation of snow and rain water, and the domes, rising from high cylindrical drums, assumed a bulbous shape.

The wife of Ivan III (1440–1505), the Empress Zoë (Sophia), who was a niece of the last Greek emperor of Constantinople, had been educated in Rome. At her suggestion the Italian architect Aristotle of Bologna was invited to improve the Kremlin buildings, and a few years later another Italian, Alevisio Novi of Milan, designed another cathedral inside the Kremlin wall.

Cathedral of the Archangel Michael, Moscow

Architect Novi, accustomed to the fantastic richness of the Milan cathedral, brought a sumptuous coloring to Russian churches. Not only did he design the first two-storied church, but, with the large shell-like decorations of the upper floor, he called attention to it. Everywhere the Cathedral of the Archangel Michael *(left)*, built in Moscow from 1505 to 1509, is filled with details favored by the late Renaissance—scallops, entablatures, pilasters, and composite Corinthian columns.

219

Cathedral of the Assumption, Moscow

The architect Aristotle of Bologna was hired to design the Cathedral of the Assumption *(left)* for the new capital at Moscow. He took the five-domed, cross-in-square plan of one of the holiest Russian churches, the Cathedral at Vladimir, and simplified its design by reducing the number of aisles to three and dividing each of the side apses into two. Round-headed panels divide the walls and mark off the interior space, giving it an Italian Renaissance feeling of balance and harmonious symmetry. In this cathedral, built from 1475 to 1479, the czars were crowned, and the interior frescoes were repainted for each coronation.

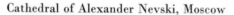

Cathedral of Alexander Nevski, Moscow

The embellishments introduced into Russian ecclesiastical buildings by the imposing Cathedral of the Archangel Michael were expanded later, with exotic effects, in cathedrals such as that of Alexander Nevski *(right)*.

Saint Basil's, Moscow   *Mella*

The most famous and familiar of the great Russian churches, Saint Basil's, was built in
Moscow from 1552 to 1560 by Ivan IV, called the Terrible, to commemorate and give
thanksgiving for his great victory at Kazan in 1552. The storming of that city and its
conquest from the Tatars gave Moscow control of the entire course of the Volga and
therefore supreme political and commercial importance.

Modern Houses of God

Modern churches everywhere show that the faith that sustains them is not frozen in the mold of the past, but is vibrant and alive in the present.

Photos: Kidder Smith

Notre Dame de Raincy *(above)*, started in 1911 at Le Raincy, France, was the first architectural expression of the new liturgical movement that began in 1909. Auguste Perret's plan recalls the old basilica.

Opposite: Saint Anna, Düren, West Germany; designed by Rudolf Schwartz

Above: Church of the Advent, Copenhagen, Denmark; designed by Erik Møller

Right: All Souls, Basel, Switzerland; designed by H. Baur

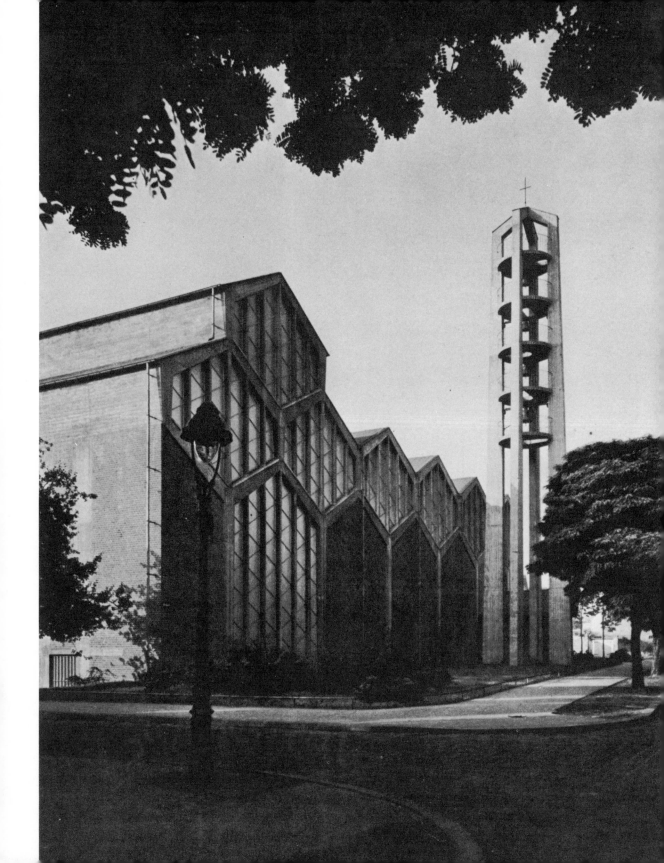

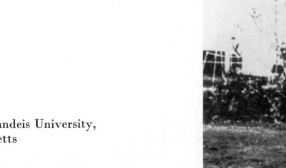

Interfaith Center, Brandeis University,
Waltham, Massachusetts

Cathedral at Ponce, Puerto Rico

Wayfarers Chapel in Palos Verde, California; designed by Frank Lloyd Wright   *Graphic House, Inc.*

Mella

Le Corbusier's triumph of simplicity and silence at Ronchamp, France *(above)*, was consecrated in 1955. It is, in the opinion of many, the greatest modern house of worship anywhere in the world.

Opposite: Meditation Room, United Nations, New York: fresco by Swedish artist Bo Beskow

ACKNOWLEDGMENTS

Photo credits appear with the illustrations throughout the book, except in the case of photographs supplied by the following sources, to whom general acknowledgment is made:

Archaeological Survey of India
Asia Society, Inc.
Austrian State Tourist Department
Austrian Tourist Foto
Belgian National Tourist Office
British Railways
British Travel Association
Department of Archaeology, India
Deutsche Zentrale für Fremdenverkehr
Direccion General del Turismo

ENIT
French Government Tourist Office
Government of India Tourist Office
Information Bureau, Royal Afghan Embassy
Information Service of India

INTO
Irish Tourist Association
Kentucky Division of Publicity
Polska Akademia Nauk Instytut Sztuki, Pracownia Fotograficzna
Press Information Bureau, Government of India
Puerto Rico News Service
Schweizerische Zentrale für Verkehrsförderung
Studio Editoriale Fotografico
Swedish Tourist Traffic Association
Swedish Travel Information Bureau
Union of American Hebrew Congregations
United Nations
Yugoslav State Tourist Office

INDEX